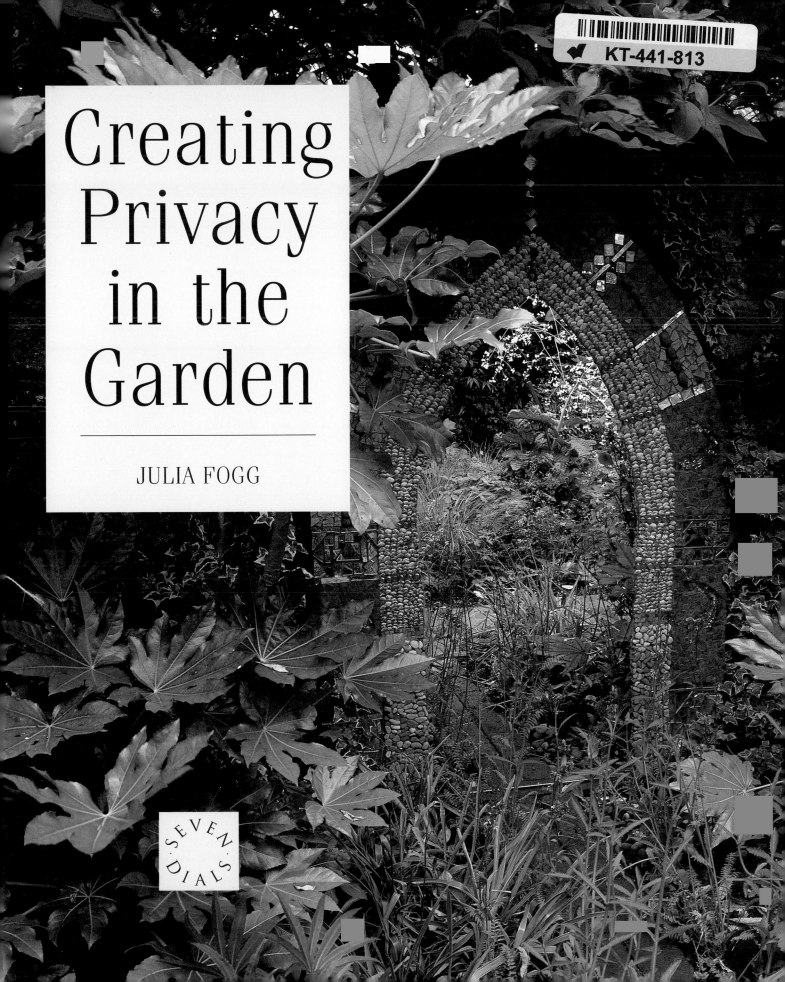

Creating Privacy in the Garden

JULIA FOGG

SEVEN·DIALS

For Mollie, with love.

First published in the United Kingdom in 1999 by
Ward Lock

This paperback edition first published in 2000 by
Seven Dials, Cassell & Co
Wellington House, 125 Strand
London, WC2R 0BB

Distributed in the United States of America by
Sterling Publishing Co., Inc.
387 Park Avenue South,
New York, NY 10016-8810

A CIP catalogue record for this book is available
from the British Library

ISBN 1 84188 099 X

Designed by Chris Bell
Illustrations by Alan Hughes

Printed in Hong Kong

Frontispiece: Sparkling light and a tantalizing focus have
been added to a shady wall by setting a simple mirror in
a frame of translucent mosaic fragments, beads and stones.
the starry white flowers of the great kale, *Crambe cordifolia*,
are captured in the reflection.

Contents

Introduction

'PRIVATE', 'not on view', 'relaxed', 'a place where I can feel entirely at home' – these are the types of attribute that people mention to me when they are discussing what they want from their gardens, even if they have only a tiny courtyard in the middle of a city. Gardens in which people feel uncomfortable, overlooked, threatened by noise, too cold or too hot – basically, a part of their home where they do not feel at home – are unacceptable today.

Generally, we expect a lot from our back gardens: we like to eat and entertain there when the weather is fine, but they are also the places where we hang out the washing and store the rubbish bins; they may also be children's playgrounds, plant nurseries and sources of home-grown fruit and vegetables. The front garden becomes a sterile area, providing a functional space for the car but offering little that is aesthetically pleasing and saying timidly: 'this is us, but don't look too closely.' Roof gardens are abandoned as too exposed, both to inquisitive eyes and blustering winds, while basement courtyards often become little better than junk yards. Can a private haven be carved from all of these?

We all have our own idea of what constitutes a peaceful retreat, and what would be one person's idyll probably wouldn't fit the bill for another, although both might define it in similar terms. In one person's mind's eye might be a picture of the snug warmth of brick walls, the sound of trickling water and a hammock in which to gaze at foliage fluttering overhead; another person might have a vision of a secret glade away from habitation, a very quiet space, without flowering plants or running water or any obvious garden feature – nothing but silence.

What these dreams do have in common is the expression of a desire to have a breathing space, where we can withdraw into solitude. We are very happy to look out from our refuge, but we do not want to be looked at, for unless we feel relaxed in our retreat, we won't use it with any pleasure. No two people's ideals are the same, but by working with what we have and what is realistically possible, we can hope to create a garden with a sense of serenity, of magic.

△ Traditional-style components furnish an intimate nook and counterbalance the dynamic forms of the hosta, ligularia and hydrangea.

◁ Sound and light are used to extend the use of this private 'nest' with rustling foliage, bird song, wind-chimes and small bells to mask urban noise, combined with discreet lighting from a variety of sources.

Socially, our reasons for enclosing ourselves in courtyards and green walls have changed little since primitive humans sheltered and protected their territory to keep out predators. The first step towards a garden was probably a clearing in the forest, near water and with a flora of native species. As humans made their living from the land, they staked out boundaries and organized enclosures, and the concept of private land evolved.

In the Middle Ages the world was a harsh place with little privacy. Castle walls kept enemies at bay, but within those walls lives were conducted much as they would be in a market place, busy and communal. An enclosed garden was a sanctuary, where nature could be enjoyed without fear; it was a place for specific pleasures and for secret trysts. Delicate and feminine, these tiny retreats were host to singing birds and twining roses. They were enclosed, romantic places, places for romance. A key was needed to unlock the prize and enter – those high, white, battlemented walls within which the Virgin in the Bower of medieval art held court were both real and symbolic.

Allowing for the evolving scheme of our lives, with its changing tempo and wider horizons, is this simplistic image still everything we aspire to: our own patch, our tiny piece of paradise where we feel secure and unthreatened? We still seek cloistered protection from unsociable neighbours and the busy outside world. This should not remain an unattainable dream, but how can we turn it into reality?

Imagine sitting in the middle of a field. It's pleasant occasionally to do this and we enjoy the sense of space, but after a while we start to fidget – we want to explore the wider landscape or retreat back to the shelter of a hedgerow or the canopy of a neighbouring oak. In effect, we need a reference point. We like a background, and we function better against a backdrop. Restaurant staff will tell you that the customers who are seated at tables around the edge will stay longer, eat more and tip more generously than those sitting at island tables. The food is the same, but an indefinable sense of security and privacy is missing from the 'exposed' centre of the room. So, although screening out unpleasant effects of the environment does not necessarily mean throwing up tall, prison-like walls, it usually requires some sort of backcloth. This might be an entire boundary fence or just a colourful sail rigged at an angle to define a private area.

There are also degrees of privacy. You may need a shield from a busy road and too many neighbours, you may want a sheltered plot for growing flowers and eating out, or you may long for a quiet corner in which to enjoy the winter sunshine. Privacy may mean having a secret arbour where you can hide, albeit temporarily, from general family life or it may, following the ancient saying, mean having 'a place private enough to make love wherever one fancies'. Whether you decide to play with hedges and screens, excavate hollows and form mounds or experiment with movable screens and distracting focal points, circumstances alter – families grow, the environment changes, requirements change their focus – so a secluded garden needs to be able to adapt and evolve.

Your garden has to suit you in terms of your requirements. Otherwise, to be blunt, it's useless. If we simply aim for function, however, a garden may be convenient but will lack character. By looking at the issue of secluded gardens as a whole – turning negative aspects into positive features and drawbacks into advantages, capitalizing on existing assets by introducing materials that overlap and interweave for overall harmony, concentrating the eye on what is within the site and so mentally blotting out encroaching nuisances – an enclosed space can be shaped by the imagination.

Life can be simple and you can have what you need, not what you are told you need. Gardens do not need flowers, just as it is not obligatory to furnish your house with carpets and curtains – you can use other forms and materials if you wish. Successful gardens reflect the personality of the owner; they may reflect fashion, but they need not be standardized. Nevertheless, on the eve of the next millennium, we are still aimlessly wandering around in the conservative world of lavender, billowy roses, topiary and off-the-peg trellis panels. Remember that there is more to life than mass-market products from the nearest garden centre. In garden terms we are steeped in preconceptions that result in mongrel gardens, which have no understandable scale or character and which bear no relation to our lives. We wear modern clothes, use modern products in our modern lives and even architecture is stripping away non-essentials and pastiche. I'm not advocating modernism for its own sake, but one of its ideals is a clarity of thought in looking at essentials to help you meet the requirements of the brief that you draw up for yourself.

The aim of this book is to offer practical suggestions and solutions that are simple to execute but that have style and quality so that you can create an individual private garden, whether it is on a city rooftop or in a secluded corner of a larger plot. This does, of course, include providing screening and shelter, but it also encompasses the other issues that come naturally into play as you achieve a harmonious, well-balanced garden. The result should be as private as necessary, as attractive and practical as possible; a garden that pleases the eye and lifts the spirit, so that you can slip away, close the gate fast behind you on life's noise and bustle and enter your own Arcadia.

1 SEEING THROUGH NEW EYES: ASSESSING AND PLANNING

WHETHER you seek to improve the level of seclusion in an existing garden or to adapt a specific area to create privacy or whether you are starting with a clean sheet, there are some simple practical questions to ask yourself before you embark on making any changes:

☐ What is causing the lack of privacy?

☐ Does the whole area have a problem or just certain parts?

☐ Are there positive aspects I am undervaluing?

☐ How would I wish to use the space if things were remedied?

This process of assessment, of finding out what you have, can inspire you to move off at tangents and may encourage you look at your garden in a new light. All the information you gather is interrelated and will fall into place when you start to make decisions about the atmosphere or type of private space you want to create – how comfortable, how exotic, how scented, how cool, how natural. By the time you reach the end of the process, you may have built up a mental picture of a secluded seating area, screened from wind and the neighbours and sited in a previously ignored corner, or you may be inspired to develop a basement area into a shady, perfumed arbour, well-clothed with climbers during the summer.

Pinpointing the problems

Are you on view from specific buildings or from neighbouring gardens when you venture outside or is it just that you have a sense of being overlooked? Just knowing that there is a housing estate beyond the boundary can be as intrusive as being physically on view. Or is your privacy invaded by sounds of one kind or another? Noise, particularly if it is a constant background, is often overlooked when people try to analyse why a garden or a backyard or a balcony feels unsettling and uninviting.

You will also need to consider whether this lack of privacy is felt year-round or is limited to predictable times of the day or to certain seasons. The ideal solution for a pocket of green surrounded by tower blocks will be quite different from a scheme for a country cottage plagued by walkers and tourists peering over the hedge on summer weekends.

Assessing what you have

The message is, therefore: get outside and look afresh at what you have. Take time to review the plot from every angle, including diagonally from corner to corner and from standing and seated positions. Note the obvious items that impinge on your privacy and think about the atmosphere and 'feel' of all parts of the space.

Make a sketch plan on which you can note all the positive and negative aspects. Hunt out any photographs that have been taken at other times of the year and at various times of the day to remind yourself of the radical changes that come with different seasons and different levels of light. Your photographs might show that tree

△ Ornamental grasses have been used to create low-level screening on this roof garden. The upright feather reed grass (*Calamagrostis × acutiflora*) along the perimeter successfully filters the breeze, while the contrasting, rather arching habit of the fountain grass (*Pennisetum alopecuroides*) is subtly exaggerated by the curves of the container.

◁◁ The simple division of the space within a rectangular plot has created an inward-facing seating area. The fig tree and arbour on the right merge to provide some dappled shade over the path.

Make a sketch plan of your garden showing all the existing features

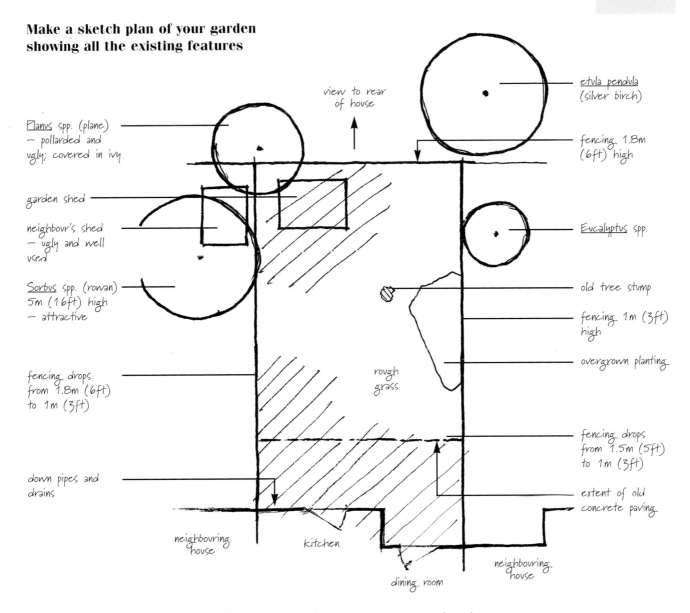

canopies and planting groups are effective screens from spring to autumn but that ugly neighbouring buildings or other eyesores are revealed once the leaves drop.

Photographs will also give you realistic images with which to plan the changes. Overlaying tracing paper and drawing in possible solutions will allow you to see, at least two-dimensionally, how the changes you envisage might work.

This might seem a rather basic way of proceeding, and you might think that you are already familiar with the problems. Nevertheless, assessing what you have, what you could keep and what would need altering is the start of the process. You will also need to take into consideration various climatic aspects and the characteristics of the soil. As with people, these are the spirit – the personality, if you like – of your garden, not the outward appearance, and they will make a big difference to the success of your campaign for privacy.

The shade cast by trees and other barriers varies from season to season

△ In winter the shade will be sparse although strong patterns will be cast on the ground.

△ In summer the canopy of a tree will give a wide spread of shade.

△ Deep shadows and hard, angular planes can be caused by a high, strong summer sun and can accentuate a private space.

Bear in mind that plans that may seem to work on paper do not always translate successfully into three dimensions. By using whatever is easily available – garden canes, pieces of timber, even your partner – to stand in for fences, trees, focal points, you can quickly establish the impact made by different effects in a 'hands-on' way.

Sun and shade

Most gardens catch some sun, if only for a limited period in built-up areas, and where and when it appears will play a part in the planning of your garden. Your share of sun and shade will depend mainly on aspect, but a garden can change in appearance and atmosphere quite dramatically during the day, and will differ according to season as the sun is higher in the sky during the summer months. Make sure that you capture or filter the sun to your best advantage. A screen that provides privacy may increase shade, which may or may not be welcome. Shade can be dense or dappled; it can be light in winter and heavier in summer; it can contribute to the sense of seclusion. Shade can sometimes be heavy and depressing, with a lack of air movement, and in these conditions plants are drawn upwards and become spindly in their efforts to reach the light.

Influences on temperature

Air temperatures in urban areas are likely to be higher than in the countryside, so town gardens – especially courtyards – will have an advantageous micro-climate, which will provide a cosy environment for humans and plants. This warmth stimulates taller and more luxuriant plant growth with abundant flowering and fruiting, which may be enjoyable initially but can all too quickly require drastic treatment to keep under control.

Where cold, heavy air gravitates and hangs in hollows in the lowest part of the land, it causes frost pockets in which spring-flowering trees and shrubs are likely to suffer. This effect can be alleviated by some judicious planting around the drop in level to deflect the flow of cold air.

Generally, dark, smooth surfaces are warmer during the day but colder at night. Pale, textured surfaces – such as gravel – remain cooler. You won't want a dark, smooth, sizzling hot floor to your roof garden, but you might wish to lighten a dark basement with gravel chippings.

Wind and pollution

Screening and shelter are closely linked. Open, exposed plots are usually windswept – a particular characteristic of roof gardens, where wind speeds can be double those at ground level. Lack of

◁ Siting a simple garden seat under the shade cast by the lime green foliage of a *Catalpa bignonioides* 'Aurea' creates a quiet retreat, whose secluded nature is emphasized by the informal barrier provided by the statuesque *Geranium palmatum*.

shelter is a common reason for not making use of an outdoor space, but it can be easily rectified, either with shelter belt planting where space permits, or screening with a structure that filters the wind. In a small town garden, where space and soil are precious, a manmade framework might be more suitable, taking up less space and possibly having the added benefit of giving overhead shelter from sun and rain.

Solid fixtures can cause wind eddying and turbulence, and wind direction can be unpredictable. Solid walls will certainly exacerbate wind turbulence, as will panelled fencing – until it's blown down. In towns and cities, turbulence caused by wind around buildings is a variable phenomenon. Sides of buildings can deflect strong, cold winds downwards and gaps between buildings channel the diverted airflow. Permeable planting, however, breaks the force of the wind while allowing some of the air to move through, creating far less turbulence.

Prevailing winds can carry pollution from noise and atmosphere, which are part of the downside of life today. Dense evergreen planting can filter a good deal of noise from traffic and industrial units, but noisy neighbours are more of a problem. Careful positioning of a well-camouflaged seating area, away from the direct air flow, can help to mitigate this, as can the soothing sounds of running water and fluttering leaves.

Foliage absorbs a good proportion of dust particles in urban atmospheres. Trees and climbers that have a large surface area

The micro-climate of an enclosed courtyard

Micro-climatic differences develop in contained areas, not in windy, open sites. In an area enclosed with brick, the walls will absorb heat during the day and transfer it out during the night, like a storage heater, making the courtyard several degrees warmer than the prevailing outside temperature. This is invaluable on cold nights, but it can get uncomfortably hot in the summer, and plants can scorch against brick walls.

Not only will sun-traps like this warm up earlier in spring and cool down later in autumn, they can be drier than other open areas nearby. Scent will linger longer, and such a sheltered spot will be attractive to wildlife if plants are well chosen to suit the conditions. Plants will help to lower the air temperature by providing shade and drawing the heat from the air by transpiration and evaporation, and tall, light plants such as grasses, stirred by the slightest air movement, will add a sense of airiness. However, as plants give off water vapour, in a closed-in place that receives little sun to evaporate the excess moisture, the air can remain humid and unpleasant, so fewer plants will be needed in a largely shaded area.

Shelter and screening in the garden are the opposite sides of the same coin

△ Cold air will gravitate to, and hang in, the lowest part of a site. Planting will help to filter the wind and prevent frost pockets from forming.

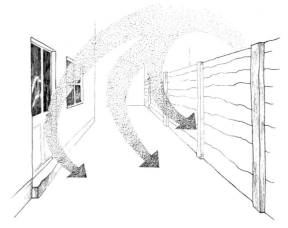

△ Solid barriers cause turbulence and eddying, as the wind is deflected downwards, through gaps between buildings and solid boundaries.

△ Barriers created by planting will filter wind and provide protection and shelter for other plants.

of foliage perform well by filtering pollutants, dust and even viruses. By their nature, they are usually deciduous but fast growing. The Plant Directory includes details of some plants that are particularly tolerant of pollution. Remember that leaves exposed to wind will lose their moisture more quickly than leaves in a more sheltered position, and large leaves will droop and suffer from windburn much more quickly than small leaves.

Soil

The plants that contribute to the success of your private spaces will only be as good as the soil in which they are growing. That doesn't mean that they all need a soil overfed with rotted manure in which to flourish – buddleias, for instance, are a good screening plant, yet thrive in the very poor soil of wasteland or roadsides.

In built-up areas it's almost impossible to be aware of the true nature of your soil without having a good dig to see how easy it is to work. This will give you immediately some idea about its structure and texture. If the house is new, it can, unfortunately, also reveal the debris from the building work and well-compacted subsoil. In cases like this you will need to import topsoil and spread it to a depth of 45cm (18in).

Like humans, plants need nutrition to survive. This is found in the topsoil and is a mix of mineral and organic material, from minute particles of rock to decayed vegetable and animal matter, broken down by micro-organisms and released back into the soil. The ideal soil has a dark, crumbly texture and smells good and wholesome, and it will reap dividends. All too often, especially in urban gardens, soil has been compacted, so rainwater runs off without penetrating and, because there are too few trees around, receives little leaf-mould to improve its organic content. If your soil sounds like this – pale, tired and powdery, without substance – you will need to build it up by mulching and adding fertilizers when you plant.

If your soil is sandy and thin, nutrients will quickly leach out, so you will need to add extra organic matter in the form of compost or well-rotted manure. Each helping – and a hungry sandy soil will need a lot – will go to improving the structure by bulking it up and will aid moisture retention. A clay soil, which will be heavy and sticky and lack air pockets, will also benefit from extra organic material, plus grit or coarse sand to improve drainage and prevent waterlogging.

To complete the assessment of your soil analysis, you will also need to test the acidity or alkalinity of your soil, known as the pH value. This can be done with a kit that you can find in most garden centres. The range of the scale varies between pH8.5,

indicating an alkaline soil, to pH4, indicating very acidic soil; ideally, you would wish to see your sample read as pH6.5 or pH7, a neutral soil, in which most plants will be reasonably content. In a larger garden you should take a selection of readings from different areas. Looking at what is already growing happily, either in your own garden or nearby, will also give you a rough idea of your soil type – bracken and rhododendrons would indicate acid soil, for example, while ox-eye daisies and lilac mean chalky limestone.

△ Using a combination of elements to maintain interest inside the garden need not result in an unsatisfactory hotchpotch. Used formally, diverse components can give a harmonious result.

There are benefits to all types of soil. Roses flourish in urban clay; while in a large garden with a wet clay soil, willows and poplars can make an enviable screen not possible in other situations. An acid soil means you can grow acers, camellias and heathers, and in a dry, gravelly soil all those aromatic, silver-leaved Mediterranean plants will thrive. Work with what you have; there's little point in trying to change drastically the characteristics of large expanses of soil. Although, as we all want what we can't have, you can, of course, create small pockets of contrasting conditions or use containers.

Accentuate the positive

Analysing with an objective eye can reveal hidden qualities of your garden waiting to be unmasked. They may not only perform a significant role by providing a focus, but also act as a starting point for generating inspiration and ideas. There is tremendous satisfaction in discovering hidden features and long-forgotten items — old stone slabs revealed under garden debris or a pool surround exposed through a mass of overgrown perennials. Existing garden buildings, even just a simple timber shed, can form the back or side of a secluded patch or even be transformed into a small summerhouse (see page 85). Recycling is always pleasing in monetary terms and provides a sense of personal achievement as well.

Look for changes in level in your site. Even the slightest drop in ground, emphasized with some upright structure as a partial enclosure, will give a sense of containment. You might feel that some sort of overhead canopy would add to the feeling of seclusion.

▽ Virginia creeper (*Parthenocissus quinquefolia*), a deciduous climber, has been used to disguise a rather ugly wall, and in winter the collection of containers will continue to provide interest and draw attention from the wall.

Trees give a sense of scale, provide shade in a hard environment, cleanse the air and provide habitats for wildlife, among many more benefits. Towns and cities need to be as green as possible, and removing a decent tree inside your garden should be regarded as a last resort. Some selective tree surgery can transform a dense canopy into a pleasing cloud of foliage and give a specimen tree a new lease of life. Even that large, gloomy sycamore at the end of your garden, under which nothing will grow, has possibilities. Think positively. Maybe it could form part of a very tiny piece of woodland, the smallest in the city, secret and special and filled with shade-loving plants that will shine through – foxgloves, periwinkle and ferns – somewhere you can escape from the phone and fax.

Neighbouring trees are permanent fixtures, and there is nothing you can do about them. However, if you're lucky, they will provide you with privacy and be attractive as well, or at least be good enough to provide a backcloth to your own choices. Careful planting to obscure your boundary line can allow you successfully to 'borrow', say, your neighbour's great white flowering cherry and seemingly enlarge your own garden to beyond its limits.

Beyond your own boundaries there will be eyesores to be blocked but also, if you are fortunate, at least one pleasing aspect that you can use as a focal point. If this is seasonal – an imposing deciduous tree, for example – you might like to supplement it with a focal point inside your garden that provides year-round interest. Conversely, the constant presence of a striking building or church spire in the distance gives you the opportunity to use plants with dramatic explosions of colour or strong winter interest as a short-lived focus inside the garden.

Turning negatives into positive attributes gives a good deal of personal satisfaction. Lateral thinking can also help. Stop thinking of your neighbour's dominating conifer hedge as an oppressive boundary and use it instead as a supporting backdrop for climbing roses. The boredom of a stretch of regular timber fencing panels may inspire you to find a colourful alternative – the outlook would be greatly improved if the panels were stained a deep moody blue and used as a backdrop for waving yellow-stemmed bamboo. Noisy neighbours can lead you to introduce moving water into the garden, thereby giving a new dimension to an otherwise adequate but perhaps dull area. Do not let the rectangular, rather stiff shape of the average plot stultify your imagination. Rectangles offer excellent opportunities to split up the space, giving linked but discrete areas for functional use and added layers of screening. Failing that, simply angling the focus of your garden so that you turn your back on an intrusion will diminish its importance.

Practical planning

When it comes to planning, be optimistic. Assume that you can successfully mitigate the outside disturbances and plan how you would like to use the garden to the full. If you enjoy eating alfresco, the space you create must be large enough to accommodate the furniture; if your gin and tonic is more enjoyable when it is drunk from where you can appreciate the evening sun, you should allow for a discreet, intimate area in the right position in your overall planning.

Finding out what you need is the practical part of the planning process, and it runs side by side with the aesthetic element
of design. Garden planning is a good deal of common sense. After
all, you live in the garden, so you know it better than anyone else.
Think about how you would like to use the garden now and in
the future.

How will your newly created private areas be used?

An arbour for one can be completely self-indulgent, but any
recreational space should have sufficient room to move with ease
– remember that you may be carrying trays of food, carrying
young children, cooking on barbecues, avoiding the dog or stepping over sunbathers.

How much room will your choice of screening take up?

If space is at a premium, a system of trellising or wires clothed
with plants might be preferable to a hedge or wall, which have an
appreciable depth to them. You will also need to take into
account access for maintenance. See Chapters 2 and 4 for the
merits of different types of screening.

△ Comforting and enclosing, the circular form is used to maximum
advantage to edge the terrace. The low retaining wall is the perfect
height for perching on.

SOLUTIONS IN CONTRASTING SITUATIONS 1

A little piece of green in the city

THE smallest outdoor areas, basements
and courtyards are, by their nature,
enclosed by the walls of adjacent buildings.
In these extreme situations, you could be
overlooked from all four sides and from
above. Some overhead screening is an
obvious answer, but how and where to
erect some light cover will need careful
planning if you are not to block out much-
needed light.

This tiny yard is dark, touched only by
the afternoon sun, and is overlooked by the
windows of flats above and by a roof garden
on one side. The owner, who likes to entertain but travels a lot, dreamed of a light,
airy courtyard that would remain attractive
all year round with minimum maintenance
and that had a certain amount of flexibility
in the layout.

Freshly rendered walls and corner
mirrors bring as much light as possible into
the area. The timber framework helps to
define the boundary upwards and the overhead screening gives a sense of privacy
without blocking any precious light. The
clematis, which thrives in such a sheltered
site, keeps its long glossy leaves all year
and in early spring the scent from the
clusters of white flowers fills this little
garden. Inserting the pots of bamboo into
planters on castors means that they can
be moved around as required.

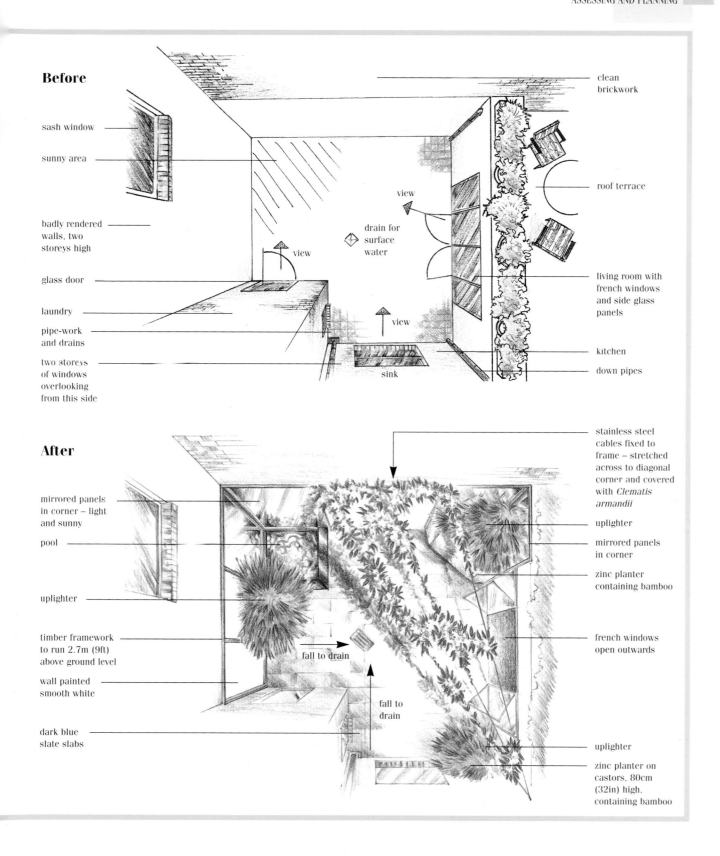

Before

sash window

sunny area

badly rendered walls, two storeys high

glass door

laundry

pipe-work and drains

two storeys of windows overlooking from this side

view

drain for surface water

view

view

sink

clean brickwork

roof terrace

living room with french windows and side glass panels

kitchen

down pipes

After

mirrored panels in corner – light and sunny

pool

uplighter

timber framework to run 2.7m (9ft) above ground level

wall painted smooth white

dark blue slate slabs

fall to drain

fall to drain

stainless steel cables fixed to frame – stretched across to diagonal corner and covered with *Clematis armandii*

uplighter

mirrored panels in corner

zinc planter containing bamboo

french windows open outwards

uplighter

zinc planter on castors, 80cm (32in) high, containing bamboo

SOLUTIONS IN CONTRASTING SITUATIONS 2

Stretching space in a long, narrow town garden

WHERE housing has been erected around a suburban grid, the problems – and potential – can be quite different. Such gardens may be of quite a reasonable size, but you could still find yourself overlooked on three sides as well as being just a fencing panel's width away from your neighbour. Hearing the neighbours' gossip from the comfort of your own deckchair may appeal to some, but even the most social of animals sometimes requires a bit of peace and quiet without having to rely on the neighbours' absence. If you are lucky, the garden boundaries will be solid fencing or established hedging, and these can form part of the background to a private area.

The owner of this house wanted private sitting areas to make the most of lunchtime and evening sun without feeling barricaded in. Although she saw its low-maintenance attractions, she did not want the whole garden given over to labour-saving paving and gravel, and scented plants and attracting wildlife were among the top priorities. She wanted points of interest in different parts of the garden and an attractive outlook from the house windows.

Discreetly splitting the garden created a 'journey' through to the rear terrace. Since this was planned as an eating area, it has shading overhead and various levels of screening to give it an enclosed feel. The bamboos provide a sense of movement, and their soft rustling helps to mask extraneous noise.

Before

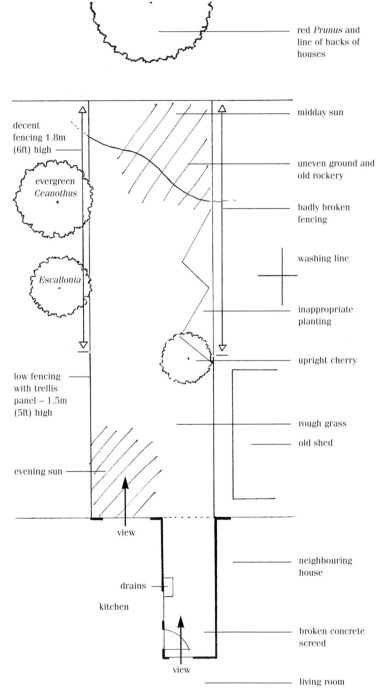

red *Prunus* and line of backs of houses

midday sun

decent fencing 1.8m (6ft) high

evergreen *Ceanothus*

uneven ground and old rockery

badly broken fencing

washing line

Escallonia

inappropriate planting

upright cherry

low fencing with trellis panel – 1.5m (5ft) high

rough grass

old shed

evening sun

view

neighbouring house

drains

kitchen

broken concrete screed

view

living room

After

evergreen screening

tall bamboos

Sorbus vilmorinii – height to merge with neighbouring planting

brick slips laid in gravel and paving to 'widen' the path

small terrace for evening sun

Malus transitoria for dappled shade

trellis screen

main terrace to catch midday sun

shrubs and climbers to mask wall

slabs through camomile lawn

storage behind trellis

water feature

trellis screen

evergreen climbers

slabs in gravel

containers

The water feature is positioned so that it is visible from indoors as well as providing a focus for the smaller seating area, which is just large enough for a chair and small table – somewhere to sit quietly in the evening sun after work. Birds are encouraged to visit the water, and rowan, buddleia and lavender are among the plants that encourage wildlife.

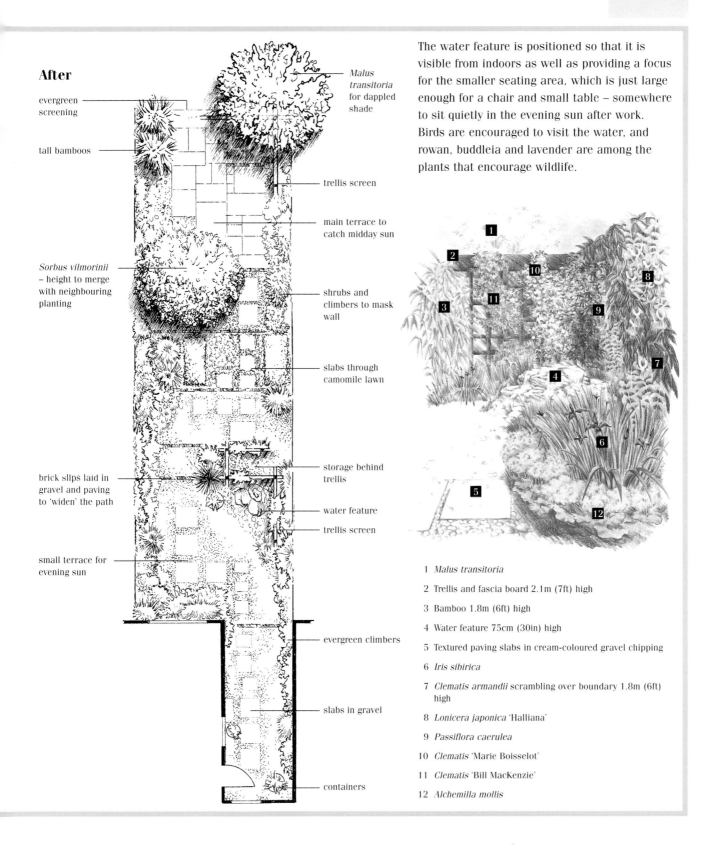

1 *Malus transitoria*

2 Trellis and fascia board 2.1m (7ft) high

3 Bamboo 1.8m (6ft) high

4 Water feature 75cm (30in) high

5 Textured paving slabs in cream-coloured gravel chipping

6 *Iris sibirica*

7 *Clematis armandii* scrambling over boundary 1.8m (6ft) high

8 *Lonicera japonica* 'Halliana'

9 *Passiflora caerulea*

10 *Clematis* 'Marie Boisselot'

11 *Clematis* 'Bill MacKenzie'

12 *Alchemilla mollis*

SOLUTIONS IN CONTRASTING SITUATIONS 3

Adding personality and privacy in a larger garden

CREATING privacy in large gardens, as with smaller plots, is aimed at keeping the outside world at arm's length. If the scenery is glorious, you will wish to see out but not be on view yourself and to choose boundaries that suit the environment and merge with the landscape. If you have the space for splendid, complementary layers of hedging and stout-trunked trees you are unlikely to want to screen yourself with thin panelled fencing, the scale of which is entirely inappropriate. Dividing a large garden is also a chance to create smaller, more intimate areas, which will lend themselves to different activities or moods.

This garden, although large, was not only in danger of being completely overlooked by a planned housing scheme but already suffered from being on show to walkers along a public footpath running along the south-eastern boundary. The owners needed planting that would

increase their overall privacy, but they also wanted to give the rather bland expanse more character and a firmer 'shape' to relate it to the house.

Where it has the space to develop, screening could become ever looser and less formal as it moves away from the house. The sweeps of decorative planting, in addition to being intrinsically interesting and providing secondary protection, create a

halfway stage between the clipped hedging that ties the garden to the house and the informal stands of trees along the boundary. The curves of yew (*Taxus* spp.) hedging that enclose part of the lawn create a quiet, reflective area while still allowing views into the open garden. Planting within this area is kept formal and simple so as not to detract from the specimen plants positioned as focal points.

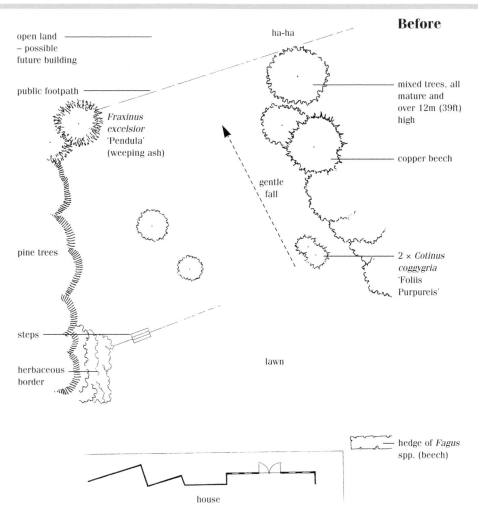

Before

open land – possible future building

public footpath

Fraxinus excelsior 'Pendula' (weeping ash)

pine trees

steps

herbaceous border

ha-ha

mixed trees, all mature and over 12m (39ft) high

copper beech

gentle fall

2 × *Cotinus coggygria* 'Foliis Purpureis'

lawn

hedge of *Fagus* spp. (beech)

house

After

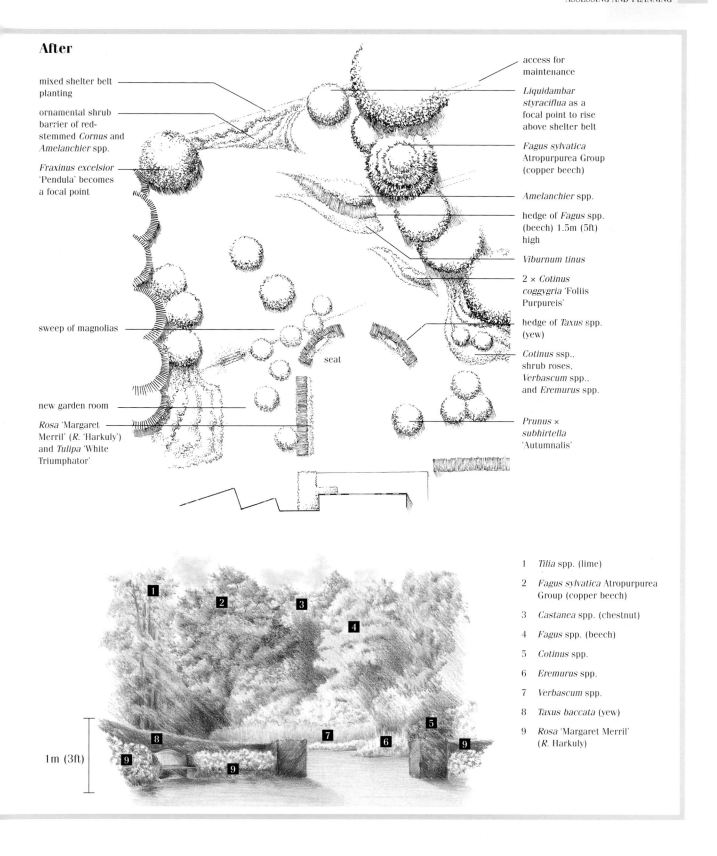

mixed shelter belt planting

ornamental shrub barrier of red-stemmed *Cornus* and *Amelanchier* spp.

Fraxinus excelsior 'Pendula' becomes a focal point

sweep of magnolias

new garden room

Rosa 'Margaret Merril' (*R.* 'Harkuly') and *Tulipa* 'White Triumphator'

seat

access for maintenance

Liquidambar styraciflua as a focal point to rise above shelter belt

Fagus sylvatica Atropurpurea Group (copper beech)

Amelanchier spp.

hedge of *Fagus* spp. (beech) 1.5m (5ft) high

Viburnum tinus

2 × *Cotinus coggygria* 'Foliis Purpureis'

hedge of *Taxus* spp. (yew)

Cotinus ssp., shrub roses, *Verbascum* spp., and *Eremurus* spp.

Prunus × *subhirtella* 'Autumnalis'

1m (3ft)

1   *Tilia* spp. (lime)

2   *Fagus sylvatica* Atropurpurea Group (copper beech)

3   *Castanea* spp. (chestnut)

4   *Fagus* spp. (beech)

5   *Cotinus* spp.

6   *Eremurus* spp.

7   *Verbascum* spp.

8   *Taxus baccata* (yew)

9   *Rosa* 'Margaret Merril' (*R.* Harkuly)

Do you require an instant barrier or are you prepared to wait for plants to grow?

You might need to consider an immediate screening device of a few light, fast-growing trees that will also cast dappled shade while a slower growing specimen is given time to form a good canopy.

Do you enjoy gardening, or would you just like to enjoy the garden?

Gardening is hard work. If it's your hobby, you will relish this. But if you want to keep maintenance to a minimum, a gentle sweep out and tidy up could be all you wish to consider. You may be among the many people who see their garden purely as a place for recreation and relaxation. You don't want to make work for yourself, so consider realistically the amount of time and effort it will take to maintain the planted areas, trees and hedging that you envisage.

How much time will you have for the maintenance?

Would it be wiser for you to spend more money initially on manmade structures that will require minimum maintenance, or would it be better to be economical and use plants to provide the privacy, although you will need to spend time in caring for them well?

Have you planned for the long term as well as the short term?

Will the proposed areas continue to be useful as your family's lifestyle changes? It would be sensible to build in a certain amount of adaptability and flexibility so that you do not have to keep rethinking the whole approach to the garden every few years or so.

Like humans, plants don't stand still: they flourish and grow; they need attention and can wither and die for no apparent reason; they also have an allotted life span – for some this may be only five or ten years. Plants also have incredibly varied rates of growth. Choosing the wrong tree, for instance, may mean that within a few years it is very much larger than you had bargained for and is a nuisance rather than an asset, or you may realize too late that you are never going to see a specimen tree fulfil its long-term potential.

The designer's perspective

Stylistically, whatever structures and boundaries we use to create privacy in the garden will mostly conform to the fundamental architectural principles – geometric shapes, the simple repetition of form and economic use of decoration. Altering our perception of a space can make all the difference. The clever use of a repeated pattern can expand a tiny urban backyard, an expanse of family garden can be reshaped to give new focal points and a cosier atmosphere, and the average town garden oblong can be concealed by discreet dividing hedges and screens to create a true Garden of Eden.

These effects do not result from the decoration, but from the shapes of the mass (the plants and solid structures), from the void (the space in which we move) and from the interrelation of the different planes. A house reaches into the garden

▷▷ A glorious profusion of perennials and annuals brings the countryside into an urban garden. Informally enclosing the bench are lupins, catananche, sweet rocket (*Hesperis matronalis*), foxgloves (*Digitalis* spp.), delphiniums and campanula, which leisurely weave through catmint (*Nepeta* spp.), Californian poppies (*Eschscholzia californica*) and sweet williams.

Timing

Once you have a workable, privacy-enhancing plan, spend a little time working out the order in which tasks need to be done.

☐   When you are tackling the garden in stages, start with areas furthest from the house, or from the point of access to the garden; this will avoid trampling over finished areas.

☐   Think systematically and deal with the basic groundwork, which is always messy, before finishing touches are started. Excavation and soil removal, and anything that requires skips or manual labour, are also more economically performed in one operation.

☐   Remember that any conduits for utilities should be laid first, even if the cable, fittings or irrigation will be installed later. This will avoid the expense and frustration of having to dig up and re-lay paving or lawn later on.

through the continued rhythms of the architecture, which are not necessarily hard and manmade but which are created with plants that have curving, three-dimensional forms. This point is often misunderstood. In small spaces, flowing curves and organic shapes in the layout of the ground pattern tend to look constricted and unhappy simply because they do not relate to their built surroundings. It is the plants themselves that will provide the rounded forms and arching habit that will spread informality in three dimensions. In larger gardens, on the other hand, the organic link of curving paths and lawns has the space to take over visually, with tree and planting masses relaxing out towards the extremities of the garden and integrating into the landscape beyond. The ways in which specific shapes and changes in perspective can influence how we view our garden are discussed in more detail in Chapter 4.

Having considered the various influences that contribute to the garden, it's as well not to think of these items in isolation but as part of the overall plan. A relaxing environment succeeds if it has been shaped with a certain degree of cohesion in the thought and planning process. Walk through the spaces that you are planning in the garden and try to envisage the outcome. Think of the garden as a whole, even if you wish to split it up into small 'rooms'. Decisions that take into account the overall effect will avoid any elements, manmade or planted, looking out of place and inappropriate. Thinking and planning in this way will also avoid the 'fruit salad' look of features dropped in at random. A sense of harmony will result from a holistic approach.

▷ The slender trunks and light canopy of foliage contribute to the semi-enclosed feel of this secluded part of the garden. Tender and hardy perennials in containers add splashes of seasonal colour against an evergreen background.

2 DEFINING YOUR BOUNDARIES

THE boundaries of the garden are the framework within which the internal structure can develop. This framework will shut out the outside world, and it should make you feel secure, safe and enclosed. No matter what they are made of, boundaries should give you the privacy required to ensure maximum use of the garden and to provide a warm, protected background for you and your plants.

In small town gardens where space is at a premium, sub-divisions of the plot will be insignificant and your boundary will be one of the most important elements of the garden. It should be effective as a barrier without the need for any secondary vertical screening, although, since the majority of compact town gardens and backyards are overlooked, you may also want some overhead screening (see Chapter 3). In larger plots, where there is more room, the boundary still plays a major role, even if subsidiary screening evolves from splitting up the space further.

Degrees of privacy

The level of privacy you need from the outside will depend on your personality, the setting and how the space will be used. Throwing up great walls won't necessarily provide the seclusion and shelter you seek and could reduce light levels drastically. The wrong type of boundary will also make the plot appear smaller than it really is.

Where housing is dense, you may want to give priority to the busiest areas close to the house, which will be the busiest area for your neighbours as well. A complete barrier will cut out visual, and to a certain extent, noise disturbance, and your ground-floor windows and the area immediately around the house will also be well screened from next door. Continuing a solid barrier around the whole perimeter will give maximum privacy, neatness and simplicity. It might be a neatly clipped evergreen hedge or a timber screen, a sleek steel fence with some

◁◁ The reassuring character of old brick walls makes them appropriate backdrops for stately plants, such as roses and foxgloves.

▷ Thickly planted square trellis makes an effective solid boundary where space is limited. The ivy *Hedera colchica* 'Dentata Variegata' is the perfect accompaniment, being similar in tone but providing a contrast in texture.

detail in the panels or a slim concrete block wall finished in subtle chalky pink, apricot or yellow to lighten a narrow passageway.

Where town gardens meet back to back or butt up to no-man's land, you could seize the opportunity to borrow a patch of the garden or landscape beyond. Even if this is just a rough scrubland, the introduction of slim trees and appropriate planting on your side can make your garden appear to expand into it, apparently threading and weaving into the beyond.

In a more suburban or rural environment you may wish your perimeter screen to be only slight, outside disturbances permitting, to make the most of attractive views and to allow the landscape to merge into your garden. This suggests a less solid boundary of timber or metal open fencing or deciduous hedging – just enough to keep nuisances out and pets and children in. Rather than relying on the boundary to provide privacy, smaller secluded areas could then be created within the garden (see Chapters 4 and 5).

Choosing the right type of boundary

Whatever the style, boundaries should have a sense of rhythm and continuity and be encouraged to wrap themselves completely around the plot. The scale has to fit in with the house, whether it is containing a large country house or a small cottage.

For much of the year the garden will be viewed from just the house windows, so the first step is to visualize the horizontal and vertical forms as pure geometry, without decoration, to identify the heights and widths of boundaries that look comfortable. Remember to do this sitting down as well as standing up. Think about the width different types of boundary take up. Will a wall encroach into the available space too much? Will there be room for access to feed and cut back shrubs or climbers in a living screen? If you are planning some overhead screening as well, would it make sense to use the boundary as a useful support? If so, it will need to be suitably sturdy.

By making sure that the boundary is in sympathy with the site and surroundings and by showing a degree of sensitivity to its immediate environment, your choice of material for a boundary will naturally fit into the style and atmosphere you wish to create, and the rest of the garden will fall into place. The key is suitability and economy in your use of the material. Simple is best. In built environments, where hard fabric is all around, think about experimenting with new materials – glass, metal and concrete, for example. In rural settings, the main chosen materials should be largely indigenous so that they will fit in naturally with the locality.

Boundaries

The ownership of boundaries needs to be identified; sometimes there is shared ownership and equal responsibility. In back-to-back town gardens each boundary wall can be the responsibility of a different household, so check on ownership with the local planning department before you rip out a hedge or erect a tall barrier. Within reason, you can treat your own walls, fences or hedging as you like, although it is worth checking on any local planning restrictions – regional policy can vary – before embarking on any major construction.

Boundaries – where they run and what is used to mark them – are too often the cause of disputes that get blown out of all proportion, wrecking what should be an amicable understanding. Even the most unattractive boundary owned by others can become, with some imaginative thought and perhaps a little compromise, a suitable backcloth for your own private space.

△ Follow changes in the level of your garden with the line of the boundary fence. Panelled fences are particularly appropriate for this type of boundary.

△ Make a feature of piers in a wall by leaving the brickwork of the piers themselves free of planting but by growing showy ornamental quinces, such as *Chaeonomeles japonica* or *C. speciosa*, against the infill panels.

Incorporating some design interest into existing boundaries will help make them aesthetically attractive as well as functional. Introduce castellations or buttresses into hedging by varying the height or width of the hedge and corbelling in the form of projections or runs and falls of different tones into brick walling; use piers and timber uprights as positive elements of a design. A simple hedge can take on another appearance and quality when it is draped with an annual or perennial climber which can withstand the dry conditions at the base of the hedge. See the Plant Directory for some suggestions.

Make any fall or change of level across the garden work with the vertical line of the boundary instead of trying to disguise or ignore it. A drop in level can be used positively as a dramatic device to encourage the eye down towards a corner of the site. A dark-stained timber fence, its line tracing the contours of the slope, would emphasize the change in level as well as providing a background with presence that shows up contrasting planting well.

The relationship of the boundary materials to the plants they contain and the aspect and conditions they prescribe is important in this context. You could end up with a sterile environment where nothing survives – privacy but no pleasure.

The colours, tones and textures of mellow brickwork, chalky stone, hard blue engineering brick or the tailored look of narrow, slatted timber fencing suggest different complementary planting. Creamy yellows and blues look better against chalky grey stone than against brick, so the roughness and character of a stone boundary wall could be shown off with cream lilies, campanulas and the burnt oranges of crocosmia and hemerocallis – bear in mind that warm oranges, pinks and creamy white need a good solid background. Modern architectural styles of fencing balance well with strong, large-leaved plants such as the variegated ivy *Hedera colchica* 'Sulphur Heart' or Japanese hydrangea vine (*Schizophragma hydrangeoides*). Considering the harmony between plant and backdrop can lead to some particularly striking results – a Japanese-style fence of paired bamboo stems interwoven with living plants is a lovely use of the same material in two different forms.

Introducing textures and colour into a constructed boundary and using foliage that has a complementary habit to overhang or clothe solid walls and fences will avoid any sense of claustrophobia. Think about types of foliage on the flat surface of rendered walls or a strong textural plant contrasting with the hardness of brick. Exploit light and shade – any planting on your boundaries can brighten and bring them to life with the play of sunlight through leaves, especially against a smooth surface. The overall effect will begin to build up, and the boundaries will no longer be seen in isolation but as part of the complete picture. As a bonus, you will be max-imizing every inch of planting space – and, as every plant enthusiast will tell you, a garden never has enough room for plants.

Despite their appeal, plants aren't obligatory. Some outdoor rooms, especially town and city backyards, are designed with just clinical and beautiful hard materials as a simple, sculptural statement. Any fuss would destroy the effect. The boundaries of such areas must be immaculately finished, with any detailing or fixings perfectly integrated, just like a well-tailored coat that needs no accessories. Style is all.

In their contribution to privacy, therefore, boundaries can be understated back-drops or regarded as a horticultural asset or treated as features in their own right.

Solid boundaries

A solid boundary gives a feeling of strength and is the ultimate barrier, in visual terms, for those on the outside, giving an imposing outer skin to a plot. Room needs to be allowed for some, such as stone walls, but others, such as a contempo-rary metal barrier, are spatially economical. Solid constructed boundaries like these do the job of screening from the moment they are built – hence their appeal. They are, however, expensive to construct because of the amount of material used and the labour needed to build them, although they can be relatively maintenance free and should have a long life. Solid boundaries will be inclined to create wind tur-bulence rather than filter the wind, so they are not always the best choice if you need your boundary to provide shelter as well as privacy.

Stone

Stone walls can have a rustic charm, but they can also be grand and imposing. They sit easily in any situation where the stone is indigenous because the tones and colourings are nature's and, as a building material, stone has similarities with human beings: no two pieces are the same. Again, this is part of its appeal. It is a strong,

◁ Natural materials should be handled with respect. A dry stone wall requires only a hint of planting – white saxifrage and compact, inky blue *Iris germanica.*

enduring material, but when it is used to build a perimeter wall, you will need to allow for a width of at least 45cm (18in).

Construction methods vary according to the strength, height and setting. Dressed stone of a uniform shape and size (ashlar) is commonly used where the finished effect (either rough or smooth face) is to be less rustic. Ashlar is invariably mortared and suits an urban setting where life is brisk and business-like. Mortared stone walls are also strong and are therefore useful where a high barrier is necessary. A more relaxed treatment, with joints left open, perhaps for planting niches, is more fitting in a rural environment, where life is less frenetic and there is less need for tall boundaries.

The size of the individual stones needs to fit the scale of the walls you are building. All natural stone walls, mortared or not, have larger units at the base, with the size decreasing gradually towards the top. For stability, such walls should also decrease slightly in width from the base up. Walls can be constructed in regular layers or courses, with selected stones of similar thickness and varying length, or randomly coursed, using tying stones or 'jumpers' to span the course and give strength. The grain in the stones should always be laid on the horizontal to prevent weathering.

Stone that has been left unshaped after quarrying is referred to as rubble (not to be confused with builder's rubble). Mortared rubble walls have different effects, depending on the type of mortar and the width of the joint. They are better coursed and need a coping, an overhanging top layer, to prevent seepage of water and consequent deterioration; this coping can also be a deterrent to intruders if it is made of flattish stones placed upright. These mortared walls have a substantial presence; they almost demand respect and therefore sit well with a building of stature and in exterior areas where an imposing barrier is the objective.

An unmortared rubble, or dry stone, wall can vary in appearance from quite lumpy to extremely beautiful. It is less strong than a mortared wall, and as a boundary material it suits a setting in a reasonably open environment, where you like to tuck yourself away from the climate and other outside factors. It would be inappropriate to consider this type of walling in an environment where the stone is not indigenous, so it is best limited to areas where the stone is a local material and consequently the necessary building skills are available. Keep to one type of stone unless you are both confident and talented – mixtures of slate, limestone and granite can be wonderful, but, frankly, you need to be quite an expert to produce walling that pleases the eye and is safe.

Brick

Brick provides a snugness that is unparalleled. Tall brick walls are imposing, their firm, upright face efficiently cutting off the rest of the world. They are especially useful in built-up environments, where they integrate well with the fabric of a city or town and take up less space than, say, a hedge.

Bricks can have a wide variation in tone and surface texture. They are also exceptionally versatile, forming unembellished barriers and backdrops, comforting sweeping curves or staggered segments. If your house is built of brick and has a traditional feel, some pattern or detailing that echoes a feature in the house walls

◁ To understand the importance of a fresh finish to walls, imagine this courtyard corner if the brickwork had been left in its natural state.

▽ Contemporary brickwork can have a pleasing simplicity. Incorporating the slightly protruding courses provides shadow lines that are an integral part of the overall scheme.

would give a feeling of harmony. Various bonds, coloured mortar and different types of bricks can be used to add interest and personality. I am particularly interested in using glossy, ceramic bricks, which come in many colours, to contribute to a modernistic and contemporary feel. These work well as a contrast to strong architectural forms of planting shapes, in small plots that capture the sun, or as part of a large boundary screen where you are using the wall as an effective feature in its own right.

The choice of bricks and the way they are laid can be used to lead the eye either away from an intrusion across the boundary or towards a feature. This way of creating a subtle and successful illusion depends on using coloured or contrasting textures in the layers of brickwork and integrating them to thread along the course. A contrasting course could form a staggered or curved line that sweeps around to wherever you desire. I have seen this trick applied successfully by using bricks like coloured ribbons, wrapping and tying the boundary walls to the building, cosseting and enclosing.

Boundary walls should be two bricks thick for strength and scale. A single-brick wall should not be higher than 90cm (3ft) and will need piers as supports, but such a wall will still have a tendency to appear thin and look uncomfortable over a long, straight stretch.

▷ The curved edge of the border exaggerates the rhythm of the crinkle-crankle wall and draws the eye down into the garden.

Walls are actually stronger when they are curved or staggered back and forth. Serpentine walls have greater stability than straight runs and are more economical in the number of bricks used than straight walls of similar length. Originally built as a support and backcloth for trained fruit trees, these wavy walls – sometimes charmingly called crinkle-crankle walls – make interesting front boundaries where they can be admired from both aspects and space is not a problem. Plot their shape by establishing a section of the circumference of a circle and repeating it in a series of reverse curves.

Bricks absorb heat slowly and retain it for a long period, contributing to a warm, cosy background, but watch out, as foliage on a sun-baked brick surface can scorch and look very wretched in extremely sheltered situations (see page 11).

Concrete and other materials

Concrete is an adaptable material and much more promising that it may at first seem. Used in boundary walling, it can be formed into piers or supporting corners of varying widths and thickness or used to make secluded seating areas within a perimeter wall. Concrete blocks provide an inexpensive, basic solid boundary, which can be constructed quickly. The blocks can be used to form walls with angular, jagged tops, making access from the outside difficult, or fluid, encompassing walls in modern, organic shapes. Finally, it can be disguised and finished in many ways.

Colour washing the surface brings life to any setting, and it requires little imagination to find ways of creating suitable treatments for block walls smoothly rendered or with a rough stucco finish, textured with an added aggregate to look modern or aged, or with other materials – mosaic, tile, stone or glass – applied as a finish. Or use the walls as a plain vertical surface covered with hanging pots of geraniums, like the walls of a *patio* in a medieval Spanish town. A wall like this will need some form of coping along the top to prevent deterioration – brick, stone, tile, treated timber or metal are all suitable.

Poured concrete walls are constructed *in situ* with shuttering, and they usually incorporate reinforcing rods and strengthening at the corners. Any shape is possible, and the surface can be imprinted with a strongly figured material to give, say, the effect of rough timber. Hammered indentations can disguise the base material completely.

A more natural variation on a concrete wall is provided by rammed earth. Moistened earth is pressed and compacted inside a timber frame, which is removed when the body is dry, and finally plastered. Rammed earth walls suggest an oriental style, and can be curved or tinted and have delicate openings and carved doorways in any strange, wonderful shape you wish – more uplifting, perhaps, and certainly more individual than concrete blocks.

Decorating solid walls

Walls of all types can be adapted and decorated to enhance their sense of containment and interest. Where space is limited and buildings are close together, the solid boundaries needed to ensure complete privacy may also restrict natural light and be a little oppressive. Enlivening walls with a suitable finish or treatment heightens their interest and can mask negative points as long as there is simplicity in the overall effect and the correct proportion of the main material is maintained.

The tiling on walls in Portugal or those amazing mosaics of broken ceramics that Gaudí used to cover all manner of buildings can be a colourful source of inspiration, while applying a pattern with shells, shiny stones or pebbles can bring interest to a dark basement wall.

△ When a wall becomes an art form – exotic, lively and amusing – the elements that accompany it should be understated.

◁ Decorative elements can be built into a plain wall as well as simply hung on the surface.

△ This rendered and painted wall simply glows. Warm colours will brighten as well as bring a comforting feel to an otherwise plain surface. The black form of lily turf (*Ophiopogon planiscapus* 'Nigrescens') nestles in a container at the foot of the wall, while the angular leaves of the yucca stand stark against the background.

Glass blocks make a solid but translucent 'window', which will relieve a hard mass and obscure all but vague shapes. Used as part of a boundary against a mass of foliage, their effectiveness is compelling.

Washing simple coloured tones over brickwork will relieve a gloomy wall – Pompeian red, for example, would be the perfect foil for cream and green planting. Freehand painting – whether geometric designs, primitive-style art inspired by the first cave paintings or a complete mural – can transform a plain wall.

Alternatively, rows of shelves stacked high with pots of favourite plants bring life to a dull situation.

Green walls

Growing plants against a solid boundary will help to absorb noise, and the sound of rustling leaves will also help to mask sounds. Plants soften the hard lines of built, possibly unattractive, barriers and help them to merge in with the landscape beyond, while creating a private haven within. Such 'green walls' not only improve the quality of life by absorbing pollutants and noise but help to extend the natural environment into urban areas, so that house walls, garden walls and fences become the cliffs, mountainsides and hill slopes of a city. They have a visual and psychological benefit and we should learn to use them as an active building material and treatment in their own right not just as an afterthought.

Green walls can provide a simple elegance, remaining green all year, or they can be planted for seasonal colour. Think about the effect you require and the attributes of the plants for the location – mixtures and combinations of flowering and foliage will give changing interest through the year.

Many people worry that climbing plants will damage surfaces, especially that they will loosen the mortar and ultimately make the wall unsafe. However, if the construction is sound, a green surface can actually protect against weathering. In summer, many species of climbing plant raise their leaves in response to the angle of the sun, shading the surface. They also keep the walls drier, because rainfall is shed from the leaf surface on to the ground, so the harmful effects of acid rain cannot penetrate and damage underlying building materials.

Some rainwater is held on leaves longer than it is on man-made materials, so the slow evaporation from vegetation against walls also assists in cooling buildings, making the temperature more comfortable. Many hardy evergreens thrive on shady walls, and these can help to keep buildings warm in winter because evergreen climbers will trap a layer of air and give some insulation. Deciduous climbers that enjoy a sunny aspect, such as virginia creeper (*Parthenocissus quinquefolia*), climbing roses, wisteria and jasmine, will insulate in summer but allow sun to warm walls in winter. On west-facing walls climbing hydrangea (*Hydrangea anomala* subsp. *petiolaris*), honeysuckle, clematis and Chinese virginia creeper (*Parthenocissus henryana*) will thrive.

There are benefits for wildlife as well, because climbers and wall shrubs provide places to rest and feed for many small mammals and offer sites for nests and roosts for birds, which are especially valuable in towns and built-up areas.

Providing a framework

Some plants, of course, can support themselves. Self-clingers such as ivy and virginia creeper can manage with nothing more than a textured surface to cling to, and plants that climb by spiralling upwards around an object, such as jasmine, chocolate vine (*Akebia quinata*) and annual climbers, will happily snake up timber battens,

Planting near a wall

Living conditions for plants against a wall will be difficult, with extremes of temperature and considerable dryness at the base of the wall. The planting on sunny walls will absorb more moisture than on shady ones, and dry out more quickly; more luxuriant growth will be achieved against a shaded wall. Walls absorb ground water, leaving a very dry strip at their base. The width of a wall's foundations will also leave only a thin layer of soil around the base, and that will soon become starved of nutrients. The soil's poverty is exacerbated by the 'rain shadow' in the lee of the wall, which means much of the rain may never reach parts of the soil close to a wall. To make things worse, dew seldom occurs close to warm, sheltered buildings, denying the base of a wall yet another source of moisture.

To give a plant the best possible start, dig out an area 45cm (18in) away from the wall and to a good depth – some climbers, such as clematis, like to have their roots some 60cm (2ft) down in the ground. Leave any broken crocks, brick or rubble at the base of the hole, fill in half the pit with subsoil and compost or well-rotted manure, place the plant's rootball in position and backfill with a good quality topsoil. Water in well.

Tender stems might need support between soil level and the trellis – use a short piece of angled cane, firmly anchored in the ground, to tie the stems to. A small cylinder of netting around the base of the stem will give protection from strimmers, scrabbling pets and keen gardeners with hoes.

◁ Climbing plants festoon a trellis to form a harmonious green wall. The golden-leaved hop (*Humulus lupulus* 'Aureus') twines its way through a variegated Persian ivy (*Hedera colchica*).

Making a frame

A substantial and functional framework of treated timber, with lattices of, say, 30 × 30cm (12 × 12in), will provide a strong climbing frame. If possible, leave a gap of about 20cm (8in) between the latticework and the wall to gain full advantage of air flow and to mask any down pipes. If it suits the architecture better, a steel frame makes a finer but still very strong support. To tie in the plants, use strong string or raffia that will not cut and damage the stems as they grow and that will decompose within about 18 months.

If you can, put up the trellis so that it is removable in sections. Plants can then be peeled back, laid down and replaced with as little disturbance as possible when you need to carry out any building maintenance.

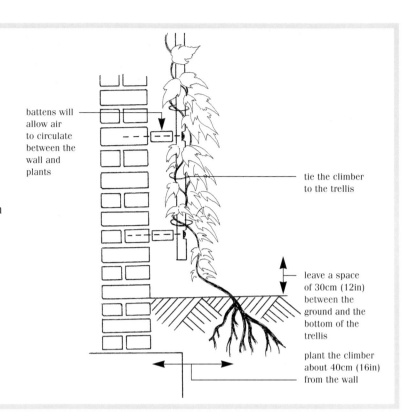

battens will allow air to circulate between the wall and plants

tie the climber to the trellis

leave a space of 30cm (12in) between the ground and the bottom of the trellis

plant the climber about 40cm (16in) from the wall

trellis, cable or plastic rope. Plants that hold on by clinging petioles (leaf stalks) – vines and clematis, for example – will need a gridded framework, and the rambling and adventurous woodier stemmed plants, such as roses or trained wall shrubs, will need a strong latticework frame that you can tie into.

Painted or stained a distinctive colour, the trelliswork can contribute to the overall style of the wall. A word of warning: don't paint the trellis white – it will quickly look shabby and ugly.

An unattractive but sturdy boundary surface can be disguised by covering it with coarse-mesh wire netting, which should be stretched tightly over a framework of heavier wire. The supporting wires can be attached to the wall by passing them through spaced vine eyes and by making sure that they are as taut as possible. Allow twiners and climbers to scramble up, then cascade down, this climbing frame to provide an almost hedge-like effect.

Solid fences

Fences of metal, timber and other woody materials can be as sturdy as stone and brick walling, although they do not have the same stature and authoritative feel. Fencing has the advantage of taking up less space above ground as well as providing a complete screen. It is useful, therefore, where conditions are cramped but not effective for absorbing or screening noise. Fencing consisting of horizontal elements will appear to stretch and widen a site, whereas a complete barrier of vertical elements will emphasize the height.

Timber can have many different characteristics and bring different qualities to a garden. Smooth oak panels, fixed to form a sculptural screen, make an expensive but simple barrier that, in a compact space, requires nothing else – it is solid, attractive, tactile and complete. Rugged, recycled railway sleepers, laid in staggered lengths for stability, will make a substantial fence, but note that you will need to provide support in the form of reinforcing rods if the fence is over three sleepers high. Such a fence, which would suit a rural or coastal setting, is a comparatively inexpensive style of barrier that merges into the surroundings. It could either be left unadorned or be mixed with a planted hedge or screen – perhaps tamarix, elaeagnus or sea buckthorn (*Hippophae rhamnoides*) beside the sea, or *Rosa rugosa*, the dwarf thorn (*Crataegus monogyna* 'Compacta') or rosemary for an inland garden.

△ Bamboo canes set shoulder to shoulder are pinned to the hidden horizontal rails of the supporting framework to provide a strong, resilient and graceful barrier.

Close-board fencing is more resilient and tougher than panelled fencing if it is treated with a stain or preservative and not left exposed. Cheaper types of interwoven or overlapping panels are only a short-term answer to creating privacy because they are visually unappealing, too thin and not resilient enough in windy areas. They will also need annual maintenance. They are useful as a stop-gap, however, while your hedge or planting belt is developing. Stained as dark as possible, even black, and associated with the strong tones of evergreen and light variegated foliage to give them some character they are passable.

Decorative finishes can transform ordinary timber. Consider not only staining or painting but also sensitive touches that imbue character. The Japanese rub the surface of timber with pumice to give a satiny finish that weathers to silvery grey, or they scour wood surfaces with sharp sand to expose the grain. Their sense of detailing is especially fine, even down to rubbing in earth to encourage moss to grow. The bottom rail of their fencing is sometimes lifted clear of the ground and set on a layer of stones, providing a visual statement as well as having the practical use of preventing deterioration.

Brushwood fencing panels, packed with bound and knotted twigs and strengthened with bamboo uprights within a framework, are a decorative alternative to standard fencing. They can have protruding poles sharpened to a point if you feel the need for extra security or the brushwood can be left clear and feathery to make a delicate, ornamental capping. This is a creative idea with simple materials and natural components that maintains a solid screen as well as merging into soft landscaping. Panels like this may be just the answer for additional shelter on a roof garden because they are reasonably permeable and yet easy to install.

Solid fencing does not have to be wooden. A crisply designed steel fence wrapping around a minimalist urban space makes a perfect slim boundary. Supporting posts will underline the neat appearance, and the panels could echo an architectural feature of the building. A specially applied paint coating finish will add colour, making a secluded frame for a city garden.

A little simple customizing of your fencing can make it serve its purpose more effectively and add personality. If it suits your circumstances, use lower sections in places, which will give you an appreciation of a vista beyond or allow neighbouring planting to form a soft part of your boundary line. Mix heights of panels to draw attention to changes in level within the garden or just to form a rhythmic pattern, or try staggered panels interplanted with clipped shrubs.

Hedges

Hedging cannot be described as solid, but it can become dense after a few years and, most importantly, it absorbs noise and is permeable. A combination of a cost-effective, constructed barrier and ultimately dense, evergreen hedging gives you the best of both worlds.

Clipped hedges as boundaries can be either kept slim or battered – that is, shaped so that they narrow upwards from the base and allow light to penetrate the bottom growth. The top width can be cut to an angle to prevent snow from settling and weakening the hedge. Realistically, a boundary hedge will need at least 60cm (2ft) growing width, plus sufficient space for maintenance and, if not for clipping, at least for mulching. It pays to leave a service path along a hedge, especially where any planted areas encroach. These areas will be dry because of the hedge roots but will provide ideal cover for wildlife.

Hedges can be planted in single or double rows. Small hedging plants called slips, usually in native hedging mixes and with beech or hornbeam, are always planted in a staggered double row so that the plants nurse each other along and grow out from the base to form a thick barrier from the ground up. The planting distances suggested in the Plant Directory will, in most cases, give a reasonable screen after five years, although some, such as box (*Buxus* spp.), can take a decade to reach shoulder height. Much will depend on site, soil condition and quality of plants. Buying larger plants is not always cost effective, not only because they are individually more expensive but because they can take longer to establish.

All hedging needs attention once a year, and some types – yew (*Taxus* spp.), box (*Buxus* spp.), leyland cypress (× *Cupressocyparis leylandii*) and privet (*Ligustrum* spp.), for instance – require two or three clips a year to keep a formal appearance. Informal hedging succeeds best with plants that have good growth near the ground and do not have a leggy habit, but bush out in a full and rounded form. Depending on conditions and your requirements, laurustinus (*Viburnum tinus*), *Berberis gagnepainii*, broadleaf (*Griselinia littoralis*), escallonias and bamboos are among the many to consider.

Hedges will not provide immediate privacy and will need a short-term outer skin to provide a solid screen, but eventually your boundary hedge can grow as high as you like – there are usually no planning restrictions provided you do not block visibility near a road.

Evergreen hedging

Dense evergreen hedging is a sensual, often aromatic method of screening. Softer than walls and fences, it is nevertheless an effective barrier, which can vary in character – clipped formally to provide architectural stature or left to grow at will to blend with the landscape. Your choice will depend on the atmosphere you wish to create and the appearance you feel you can maintain, but you will need to be patient.

Yew (*Taxus baccata*), the dignified aristocrat of evergreen screens, makes a faster screen than is generally thought and, if well watered and fed, will soon show dividends. Remember that it is poisonous to animals and should not be used as a boundary to grazing land.

▷▷ The cool greens of a mix of waxy evergreen and some variegated deciduous foliage create an intimate niche in summer. More of the wall is revealed when the weigela loses its leaves.

Box (*Buxus sempervirens*) is slow growing but ultimately very rewarding, making a dense, soft hedge of a slightly brighter hue than yew. Like yew, it has a natural formality and clips well. Both yew and box hedges can appear, after years, to have been carved by the elements, and they can be nurtured into glorious pieces of abstract sculpture. Each makes a fine hedge alone, or they grow well together.

The shiny foliage of cherry laurel (*Prunus laurocerasus*) is fresh green and pollution tolerant, but the thick stems and large leaves make cutting back hard work and you are left with ugly stem-ends until new growth sprouts. This is not a problem with the neat-leaved twiggy privet (*Ligustrum ovalifolium*) and the box-leaved honeysuckle (*Lonicera nitida*), but they will require clipping two or three times a year to achieve a thick, close-textured screen.

Most conifers make suitable hedging in the right situation – as the sunlight falls on to its clipped flanks, even × *Cupressocyparis leylandii* takes on a personality when it is sheared into angular corrugations or close columns. As an alternative to leyland cypress, and one that has the good aspects and not the bad points of that rampant and greedy plant, try *Thuja plicata* 'Atrovirens', a form of the western red cedar. The featheriness of its dense, aromatic foliage contrasts well with laurel's glossiness.

Holly (*Ilex* spp.) is a traditional and very useful hedging plant, acting as a spiky deterrent as well as tolerating pollution and shade. Topiary topknots are traditionally used as garden boundaries for all types of habitation, and in some villages almost every hedge has a mature, single-stem specimen holly, each one styled differently.

Clip holly formally or incorporate it into a loose, evergreen boundary screen, with yew, box, ivy, mahonia, elaeagnus and pyracantha. Some deciduous blackthorn or sloe (*Prunus spinosa*) will add highlights of flowers in mid-spring and purple fruits in autumn, and the combination will form a barrier with a rural feel that inhibits the most determined of intruder.

If you want seasonal interest from berries and flowers, try *Berberis sargentiana*, which gives a mass of clear yellow flowers in late spring and can be trimmed after flowering. *Cotoneaster lacteus*, which bears dark red fruits, fills out well from the base and clips to any form desired.

Deciduous hedging

Deciduous hedges have a special attribute – that of transformation. Different hedges have their own characters and will fulfil different roles. Colonnades of beech (*Fagus sylvatica*) or hornbeam (*Carpinus betulus*) have a smart appearance, fresh spring coats and warm, fluttery brown packaging in autumn and winter. They make formal hedges that fit comfortably into both urban and rural settings and that look especially glorious flowing down sloping land. As a screen, they are tactile and attractive, retaining their crinkly, dusty, brown winter foliage until late in the year. Although the base of a hedge will be dry, a thread of *Geranium ibericum* would give a pleasing highlight – a brief ribbon of rich mauve along its foot in early summer.

The dense structure of this type of hedging, when well grown, makes an impenetrable wind barrier that has a music of its own, but it is not a shelter belt for extreme situations where a thicket type of mixed species suited to the specific conditions would be the answer.

Mixed hedging

Mixed hedging is an interesting concept, and there are many possible alternatives and combinations. Such hedging suits predominately rural settings or large gardens that afford adequate space for the various shrubs to grow in their natural habit.

A mix of just deciduous species, to form a hedging screen for rural situations, can provide screening with the bonus of flower, berry and autumn tints. Copper and green beeches, combined with some hawthorn (*Crataegus monogyna*) and flowering quince (*Chaenomeles japonica*), are fine for country settings. For a more solid screen, some evergreen material is necessary – holly is a good mixer, or just add a little beech and holly to a predominantly yew or box hedge to make a patchwork tapestry. Spiny, vandal-proof shrubs will knit together as a dense mass that can be pretty as well as functional. Tall varieties of fuchsia and pink-, red- and white-flowering escallonia, olearia and the evergreen *Euonymus japonicus* make a good seaside hedge.

Your choice will depend on the soil and the aspect. Some species prefer bright light and some need a certain amount of shade. Hawthorn, common hazel (*Corylus avellana*), holly and blackthorn will form the backbone of a deciduous screen, with the addition of secondary species that suit the conditions – perhaps common dogwood (*Cornus sanguinea*), wayfaring tree (*Viburnum lantana*) or cherry plum (*Prunus cerasifera*).

Hedging in tiers

Multi layered hedges provide maximum interest and can look very smart, so if space permits try a double layer of a low hedge of one type backed by a high hedge of another for contrast. Pleached trees can be used in this way, too. Usually thought of as internal rather than boundary screens because of their bare legs, consider them instead as a 'hedge on stilts', forming the upper tier of a double-layer boundary. Deciduous trees such as limes (*Tilia* spp.) and hornbeams (*Carpinus* spp.) against a lower fence, wall or hedge will form a strong, high-level barrier all summer, and when their leaves fall a lighter, twiggy screen will remain to interweave against soft winter skies. The taller cotoneasters also train well and have the bonus of flower, fruit and evergreen foliage, although you should expect some leaf drop in early summer. Let their natural habit show and leave the top growth to flop gently down.

These species need adequate space to succeed, and they are not suitable for compact town gardens. Substitute the more easily manageable *Cotoneaster frigidus* 'Cornubia' in a smaller space, or follow the Japanese lead; they get it right again with camellia, cryptomeria and holly, used in combinations with fences and walls as true mixed boundaries.

Planting a hedge

To give your hedge the benefit of a good start, prepare a well-prepared border or trench with suitable well-rotted organic matter. Feed the plants each spring – liquid fertilizer takes effect quickly, but granular or powdered fertilizers can be either slow- or quick-release. These need to be lightly forked in over an area slightly wider than the spread of the plants, taking care not to damage the root system – some plants, such as box, have shallow rootballs, and these can be easily scorched by dry fertilizer. After feeding, top-dress with an organic mulch to keep in the moisture and to help keep the roots cool. With this good husbandry, your hedge will grow and fill out, and do its job of screening as fast and as efficiently as possible.

△ Contrasting textures form a solid, tiered barrier, with a border containing mixed planting adding a decorative layer.

FRONT GARDENS

THERE is no doubt that a hedge along your front boundary can provide a good level of privacy, and traditional hedging evergreens such as holly, privet, yew, box and elaeagnus are tolerant of pollution and soak up noise well. But a hedge tall enough to conceal may cut out a lot of light, and many hedges, it has to be said, are also boring to look out on.

△ A front hedge surmounted by topiary will draw the attention of passers-by away from your windows.

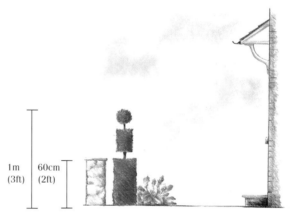

△ A clipped topiary shape, free standing behind a low stone wall, will give a more intimate feeling and would be suitable for a cottage or small town house.

1   *Hedera colchica* 'Dentata'

2   *Agapanthus* 'Dorothy Palmer'

3   *Choisya ternata*

4   *Taxus* spp.

5   *Malus hupehensis*

◁ Layers of screening will stop passers-by from looking into your garden, and a careful selection of shrubs will give an attractive, pollution-tolerant and durable hedge.

Give passers-by a talking point in the form of amusing clipped shapes or a magnificent spread of seasonal colour. Simple geometric shapes are effective, but more imaginative shapes may spur you into action. Whether you are inspired to create a line of perfect spheres or a sinuous fire-breathing dragon, people will enjoy the show – and not look beyond the display to you. Swaying grasses or a strong architectural planting can provide extra distraction for your side of the hedge.

Modern housing requires simpler remedies. Low, neat panels can be the backdrop to a riot of colourful planting that will draw the eyes of passers-by down rather than towards your windows.

It may be worth sacrificing a little of your own space to create layers of screening: light, upright trees above pencil-slim hedging to shoulder height and a spread of lower evergreen shrubs in front of that. Extend the layered effect down to a tough edging mat of ivy or periwinkle and you will have pushed onlookers well away.

Making a choice

Deciding on a style of hedge is a very wide brief, so ask yourself a few questions to help narrow down the choice:

☐ Does your hedge need to screen thoroughly all year or would you be satisfied with a semi-see-through barrier in winter?

☐ Do you require something quite tall and fast-growing or are you prepared to wait for a slow-growing hedge to mature?

☐ Do you like a tidy appearance and positively enjoy clipping or would you prefer it largely to look after itself?

☐ What other purpose do you hope it will serve? To deter intruders? To act as a windbreak?

Whatever your answers, you will still be left with plenty of possibilities. Suppose you have narrowed down your choice to a predominantly summer screen that will develop into a hedge quite quickly; you haven't got the time to spend hours clipping but you want it to be an effective barrier around your garden as well as something that will contribute some colour other than green.

A rose hedge would fulfil all these attributes, but again there are choices to be made. Do you want *Rosa rugosa* cultivars for their fresh green foliage, flowers and fat, orange-red hips; the sweetbriar (*R. eglanteria*) for its scent and jolly red hips; the Scottish or burnet rose (*R. pimpinellifolia*) for its dense tidy foliage and tough, hardy habit? Or perhaps the silvery foliage and bright orange berries of the tough, spiny sea buckthorn (*Hippophae rhamnoides*) would be the perfect answer. The lists in the Plant Directory include many more suggestions.

◁ A traditional herbaceous border relies on the supporting strength of a well-maintained hedge of yew (*Taxus* spp.). *Dahlia* 'David Howard', *Helenium* 'Riverton Gem', kniphofias and asters explode into colour in late summer.

A willow noise baffle

Where noise from traffic and industry is a problem, a live acoustic barrier can help to ease the disturbance and form an attractive planted screen. Two walls of woven willow support a cavity that is filled with a soil mix and a necessary irrigation system integrated to ensure sprouting shoots. Visually, the structure appears as a woven brown screen when the willow is dormant, transforming into a light green haze when the willow shoots in spring. This planted wall thickens up substantially in summer to form a brilliant green screen that moves with the wind. Noise is not only absorbed but the framework itself gives out its own sound of rustling leaves.

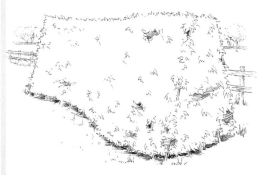

△ Weaving the willow.

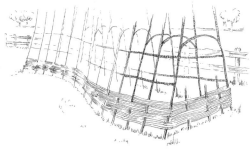

△ The willow screens make an effective sound baffle.

▷ The dynamic tones of *Clematis* 'Victoria' make a singular statement for much of the summer while it lounges across a low boundary.

Less solid boundaries

If you are lucky enough not to be directly overlooked at close quarters or if the enjoyment of a view takes precedence, a less solid boundary may give enough screening to evoke a feeling of privacy and security, while being visually less dominant. In these circumstances your choice of boundary will be to define the garden's perimeter and, especially in rural situations, to keep out animals such as rabbits and deer.

Concrete and brick screening

Lighter screens of pierced concrete or brick lose themselves visually in built-up environments while providing a degree of privacy. The texture of light and dark shadow given by a honeycomb wall is impressive as a strong feature that changes through the day, as long, angled shadow lines cast by the sun shine through the fretwork. Recesses and openings are easily made in this type of screen and it is suitable as a background to a seating area, large or small. Remember that it can act as a type of window or frame for the view beyond, so you might need to supplement it with some planting.

Open metal fencing

Metal fencing, especially wrought iron, will have to be made by a blacksmith or metalworker who specializes in this type of work. It is very fitting in a traditional setting and can look extremely attractive. Architectural metalwork can also be suited to contemporary designs, for fencing and gates, when it is formed into curving wave patterns and moulded undulations. These can then be painted to emphasize either strange and wonderful patterns or more traditional elegant shapes.

Powder-coated, tubular steel palisading can also be constructed to form undulating barriers around curved paths and boundaries, with the circular form of the unit emphasizing light and shade effects.

Painted, squared metal fencing, staggered and repeated, back and forth or up and down, fits well in urban settings. It gives a measure of security, because the pointed vertical bars are capped at 45 degrees, and it defines a boundary safely. The vibrant, cheerful, slatted fencing often used around schools and playgrounds makes a lively screen, too. This has potential as a no-nonsense, easy-care, domestic boundary. The smooth surface is washable, and the structure is reasonably lightweight with plastic slats infilling a steel frame. The strong colours of the plastic panels can be really attractive.

Fedges

The idea of a fedge – a hybrid fence/hedge – can be developed in a number of ways. Chain-link is utilitarian but provides a useful frame to smother with plants. Roses with a dense habit, such as the tough *R. rugosa* types (especially *R.* 'Fru Dagmar Hastrup') are ideal candidates, with their succession of crêpey scented flowers and bright hips. The sweetbriar (*R. eglanteria*) is also suitable but has a more restricted flowering period. *R.* 'Aloha' keeps on flowering and is also fragrant, while *R.* 'Alexander' will hit you with its flowering punch. *R.* 'Mountbatten' and *R.* 'Chinatown' would provide a less 'natural' effect, but mixed in with pyracantha and evergreen honeysuckles will combine into a vibrant and vandal-proof barrier.

One designer had a more exciting idea and constructed walls 2m (6ft) high of galvanized metal mesh with a water irrigation pipe woven around the top. In winter this drips to freeze around the chain-links and make a sparkling wall of ice. In spring and summer the irrigation pipe makes it simple to water an early-flowering clematis followed by a spread of morning glory (*Ipomoea tricolor*), and virginia creeper (*Parthenocissus quinquefolia*) finishes the effect with a flourish in autumn.

Open timber fencing

Used as a light screen, timber crosses the divide between urban and rural settings, adapting to a sleeker, contemporary treatment in town or a rustic look that is more suitable for the country. Timber is tactile and good to be close to. Any extra overhead screening can branch off quite naturally from this form of boundary so that you can achieve a more subtle form of privacy from an open framework, both vertically and overhead, without resorting to a solid boundary.

△ Low-key hazel rods provide a sympathetic and attractive backdrop to the carefully planted camassias, hosta, foxgloves and *Trollius chinensis* 'Lemon Queen', which emerge through a carpet of *Lamium galeobdolon* 'Hermann's Pride'.

△ Simply defining a boundary with an open framework of trellis can be all that's needed. The whimsical detailing individualizes the boundary.

△ Flutes of cut bamboo form an elegant screen. The container-grown bamboo *Fargesia murieliae* 'Simba', rocks and gravel complete the oriental image.

Slatted timber fencing provides an opportunity to experiment and play with design. The distance between, and the placement of, the slats — horizontal, squared, vertical or angled — give this type of fencing great versatility. Variety in widths and heights of the slats adds a feeling of movement that light and shadows can magnify. Narrow timbers give an elegant feel, while a rustic effect comes from a broader slat. Coloured stains, too, can exploit any effect. These timber fences require good construction to be strong and sturdy.

Ranch-type fencing has wide, horizontal timbers fixed to upright posts. You could give an existing fence more character by refixing the bars so that they stagger alternately behind and in front of the posts. Palisade and post-and-rail can be given added interest with a purposeful hit-and-miss design, with pales grouped wider apart at intermittent distances. With pig netting fixed along the base for animal security, post-and-rail is a suitably robust demarcation for rural plots, where the landscape beyond is an attractive feature.

Riven oak and chestnut rails are the most rustic of open fences. The full lengths are split down the vertical grain and the rails mortised into the posts, giving a quite agricultural and a strong visual effect. Hurdles, made from woven willow and hazel, will provide a short-term boundary fence. The frame is vital to strength and protection and means parts can be replaced easily. The handmade look is homely and appealing.

Not so rustic in feel, but a similar concept, are bamboo fences. These can be in varying degrees of refinement and density: an open framework of stout canes set in patterns and tied to posts, criss-crossed, squared, double thickness or slim and light. This strong, very oriental statement requires selective placing if it is not to look out of place. Panels of thin canes, laced and tied to form a dense but textured and light screen, are particularly suitable for roof garden shelters, where the wind needs to weave through and escape, but still ensure you have reasonable privacy.

Chestnut poles, stick fences and even pine floorboards, cut as rails, are not so specifically geographic and, therefore probably easier to place. They are agricultural in theme, but on a domestic scale. These sorts of fencing can be used as woodland edge barriers (with chicken wire infill buried deeply as a rabbit-proof defence), for family gardens where life is at a more leisurely pace and in situations where mixes of boundary structure and plants can weave in and around in a very naturalistic combination.

3 SCREENING FROM ABOVE

OVERHEAD SCREENING, whether in the form of an evocative, vine-clad pergola, a canvas sail as a contemporary awning or a bamboo screen to filter sunlight, can make a real difference to your sense of privacy in the garden, especially in urban gardens, which are particularly vulnerable to being overlooked by neighbouring flats, balconies and roof gardens. The suggestion of a ceiling, however open, is also an encouragement to treat the area as an outdoor room, where you can sit, eat, play, dream and generally prolong your enjoyment of the garden. This is nothing new, however: timber trellis for garden structures was called 'carpenter's work' by the Tudors and showed a true individuality from which today's manufacturers could learn. These garden rooms were called 'banketting-houses', as banquets were held there, with chimneys, barbecuing towers and turrets spouting up into the sky in a way that makes our barbecue areas look positively dull.

There are a myriad names for structures that provide shelter outside; everyone has their own different definition. Where overhead coverage comes from overhead beams or struts attached to the building, I have termed these 'open extensions', but they can also be known as loggias and verandas. They usually span useful, busy areas along the rear or side walls of the house and can be quite grand or, for more modest situations, simply bridge the space between house wall and boundary. In my own garden, for example, overhead rafters mask the area around the back entrance as well as the downstairs cloakroom window from next door. The ivy

◁◁ The Chinese gooseberry (*Actinidia deliciosa*) creates a textured ceiling and contributes to the privacy under this classical pergola. The combination of circles and squares is especially pleasing.

▽ Lush planting, dappled shade and a few thoughtfully placed features turn a small courtyard into a real extension of the indoor room.

◁ A compact, secluded room grows out of nothing more than some lattice panels, overhead rafters and a pot of paint.

Hedera helix 'Oro di Bogliasco' (syn. *H. h.* 'Goldheart'), which has a central splash of yellow on most of the fresh green leaves, clambers up and across the frame to provide a welcoming touch of brightness to a humdrum area.

Pergola is an over-used, pastiche term that seems to cover a multiplicity of senses. I am using it here to mean a free-standing structure designed to cover a functional space, giving sufficient overhead screening to combine privacy with the delights of alfresco living. Ideally, it should be placed to frame a view or lead the eye to a point of interest. Garden structures like this define spaces and the area around them, creating internal edges and boundaries that give extra seclusion, if only psychologically – if we feel more private then we'll use them.

Open extensions

In small gardens and backyards, overhead extensions directly off the house are economical in terms of space as well as being highly effective screening. This semi-enclosed room acts as a link between inside and the garden, a resting place where you can enjoy the best of both worlds. Made into a true extension of living space, it can draw you away from the house into the garden where, on hot days and summer evenings, outdoor eating is practical yet private.

These open extensions have parallels with monastic cloisters, where private, sheltered space was a necessary part of life, the shade aiding contemplation with nature just a few steps away. Dappled shade will contribute to the sense of privacy as well as emphasizing the brightness of light, and the quality and density of that light depends on the texture overhead. Varying patterns and a filigree of moving shadows where foliage creates a woven ceiling gives drama to a functional area, while extra constructed infill will give a denser feel and help to support rampant plants, although the effect of shadow patterns will be lost. Using deciduous climbers to clothe an open extension will provide shade for summer but allow as much light as possible through the winter.

Building to scale

The scale and proportions of any structure need to suit their position. This can only be done by eye while on site, and it is crucial to spend time getting this part of the process right.

For ease of movement and to cater for plant growth, allow a minimum clearance under all forms of overhead structure of 2.2m (7ft 6in). A clear access between uprights of not less than 2m (6ft) – with 2.4m (8ft) for preference – is a comfortable measurement that relates well to the clearance height and allows two people to walk through with ease. Remember that any adjacent planting can fill out and easily double in size during the summer.

If you plan to eat out under the covered area, you should allow for the maximum spacing of 3m (10ft) between uprights. It's always wise to measure out on site, or on a scaled plan, the size of the table and appropriate seating arrangement. Uprights have a horrible habit of being in the way unless you plan ahead.

Actual measurements will also depend on the materials you choose. Massive oak beams should be well spaced apart, but slimmer, softwood planks look better when they are placed closer together or in pairs with an alternate wider gap. The main supporting overhead beams or joists can be visually linked and given additional strength with slimmer crossbeams. Whatever their construction, overhead extensions cannot be scaled down too far, or their proportions become awkward and no amount of planting or decoration will disguise the fact.

Style and scale

The form your structure takes should reflect not only your lifestyle but the character of the house – it could range in style from rough-hewn or smooth, stout timber beams to metal sections, depending on the associated architectural style. Substantial overheads requiring strong supports are more in keeping when they are linked to buildings with a certain presence and would certainly be unsuitable for roof gardens and balconies. An informal structure of larch poles would appear to be as out of context in a city as an elegant steel extension with marine fittings would be if it were attached to a rural cottage.

Think about what suits the site rather than simply choosing what you see at the garden centre. Unfortunately, manufacturers and retailers seem to believe that the garden, as a place for outdoor living, is still set at the turn of the last century – hence those mass-produced copies of traditional elements that not only bear no relation to contemporary architecture but sit awkwardly in modern environments.

If the overhead extension is designed from the start as an integral part of the building you may have the opportunity to choose cantilevered overhead screening that projects in a clear, uncluttered sweep. It is more likely, however, that you will need to plan for upright supports. The pattern of doors and windows will determine the shape and position of the framework, so you will have to make sure that the uprights will not cut across the main view to the garden or make access awkward. Screening will also reduce the light reaching indoors, so explore different configurations and degrees of screening so that the amount of shade is welcome rather than gloomy. You may also have an opportunity to plan the interior and exterior as one unit, with linking surfaces, styles and tones of colour in the furnishings to project spaciousness and successfully merge inside and outside together.

If climbers such as wisteria and climbing hydrangea (*Hydrangea anomala* subsp. *petiolaris*) are to be part of the picture, the construction will need to be strong enough to bear the weight of the mature plant – you should think about an equivalent of a human weighing at least 57–67kg (9–10 stone). Some climbers develop into weighty plants that will demand a substantial support, and constantly having to cutting them back to keep them within bounds will destroy their character.

Overheads extensions, whether they are built as an extension or in a free-standing form, can also support other, less permanent, features if they are sufficiently strong. Hammocks and swinging seats have enormous appeal when slung below a shady bower, and they can be quickly taken down or simply tied back when not in use. Children's swings and slides can also be incorporated.

◁ These angled overhead beams need to be as uncluttered as possible to allow shafts of light into the passageway and to balance the dark, moody appearance of the canal of water.

SHELTER AND PRIVACY FOR A ROOF GARDEN

EVEN up above the rest of the world, in your roof-top garden, you could find it necessary to screen yourself from nearby lofty windows and similar gardens in the sky. You will certainly find it necessary to provide some shelter from the extremes of climate so that you can reap full benefit from this type of open-air living. Another positive aspect of using overhead screening in this situation is that it avoids the uncomfortable feeling of being perched on high. Instead, the roof garden becomes, like this one, a veritable cocoon in which to relax.

The lightweight but sturdy metal frame is fixed to the main supporting beams of the building – always get a structural engineer to check your proposals. There are curved corner braces for added stability and to give an elegant, decorative touch. The main frame must be strong enough to support any extra screening, whether trelliswork or planting, and, as here, overhead lighting. The panels of diamond-patterned timber lattice used as infill over the main seating area give extra protection from the sun, and using the same trellising to clad the low walls contributes a sense of harmony to the whole area.

Containers, sensibly sited over load-bearing walls, have the dual function of keeping young children away from dangerous perimeters and of housing plants. A vine creates pleasant shade and will not, in this exposed situation, grow into a monster. Although it will appreciate some pruning, it will still retain an interesting and sufficiently intricate structure through the winter.

Awnings and sails

Bright and breezy overhead screening that has the advantage of being temporary and therefore interchangeable is possible if you use sail fabric stretched between a metal support. This lightweight polyester comes in a range of brilliant colours, which give the delightful appearance of gauzy kites gently shimmering overhead – these can be double-sided so that the reverse side has a contrasting tone to suit a changing mood. Snappy yacht fittings – shackles and adjustable rigging screws – are suitable fastenings and fixings and allow quick assembly. Alternatively, lashing with coloured chandler's rope can make a positive visual contribution to the overall appearance. Canvas, a heavier material, can also be held in place with these methods, but it has the advantage over lighter fabrics of suiting a neat, roller blind format for a fast and smooth screen in open, breezy situations. All these materials look at home near water, but they are also suitable in urban settings where the faster pace of life seems to call for positive shapes, tones and materials.

Split bamboo or rattan screening is another lightweight option for exposed, elevated positions, although it will perish sooner than other materials. However, its permeable quality is a major advantage and as well as being a good textural complement to other materials it fits the majority of situations and it's cheap.

New ideas for screening will develop from many of the man-made materials that regularly appear on the market, and you can also pick up inspiration and advice from quite unrelated sources – ship's chandlers and bathroom showrooms, for example – as well as interior and architectural magazines.

Pergolas

Certain situations can demand that overhead screening is set apart from the main building – for example, you may wish to use screening to make a secluded area in another part of the garden or you may wish to take advantage of a particular sunny patch. A free-standing structure with overheads completely supported by uprights will provide the ceiling over a main functional component of the garden, leading out, where space allows, into other garden areas. The amount of covered space, even in a small garden, should be sufficiently user friendly to enable you to enjoy relaxing and eating out under a discreet screen.

Where every inch of space is precious, a pergola should appear to be linked to the boundary, to integrate it into the overall plan and to give an impression of unity with the surroundings while leaving as much uncluttered central space as possible.

Elbow room and home comforts

Covered eating areas need to be functional as well as attractive. Allow for adequate space around the table and chairs for general comings and goings and for chairs to be pushed back, away from the table. Storage space for essentials will make constant trips back and forth to the house unnecessary, and if possible, include in your plan electric sockets and downlighters, which can be set flush into the framework. Being able to see and converse with your guests is important, so work out a position for the barbecue that avoids scorching overhead beams and foliage without leaving the chef isolated.

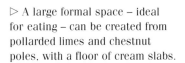

▷ A large formal space – ideal for eating – can be created from pollarded limes and chestnut poles, with a floor of cream slabs.

▽ Chestnut poles and pollarded lime trees will make an intimate space under an elegant overhead canopy.

Structures that are actually attached to the boundary might come under local planning restrictions that prescribe height limitations; it is always wise to check. An adjacent boundary fence or wall will markedly increase the degree of privacy, and choosing a corner site will give an even stronger feeling of containment.

Style and ingenuity can be without limit as long as the structure remains in sympathy with the atmosphere of the site – a traditional, domed temple in a classical setting, for example, or a modern, lightweight form with coloured glass panels and PVC screens in contemporary sur-roundings. Chestnut poles with the bark removed look good with a natural covering of pollarded limes to make a simple, softly screen-ing pergola in a cottage garden.

Materials and construction

Materials can be of one type or mixed, as long as they remain simple, sturdy and unfussy. Timber and metal are the usual fabric for piers and uprights, being versatile in formation and finish and fitting easily into a variety of situations.

Stone, brick and tiles, which are traditional-ly used as a decorative facing material around uprights, will need a concrete core and reinforc-ing rods. Stone uprights can form single columns and make a weighty base around timber sup-ports, tying an overhead structure into the stone architecture of a rural setting. Brick piers will have to be a minimum of one and a half bricks square to support strong timber crossbeams. As these vernacular materials can supply a rather monumental effect, the setting needs to be spacious and to have a suitable character.

Well-proportioned timber piers can have the rough corners chamfered to give a sculptured, refined appearance, or they can be used to construct a more open support by using four narrow, vertical shafts of timber, fixed to an internal framework, for each pier. Fat timber piers will need to be set into concrete footings, but a less substantial structure can be created by securing the uprights in metal shoes driven into the ground, and these have the advantage of eliminating problems of rot and deterioration from contact with damp soil.

Timber is the most often used material for overhead beams. The dimensions of hardwood are suitably generous to give a feeling of security as you relax beneath, and with the grain exposed it is full of character, although hardwood is costly in comparison to softwood. Softwood needs to be treated or prepared and can be stained, making a more than adequate substitute.

Overheads can seem to be attached to the building when they are supported by brick corbelling or by a notched crossbeam attached along the length of the wall. Crossbeams can be jointed to give a smooth finish or partially jointed to give a more interesting shade pattern. Overhangs usually look better when they are left proud, with the ends shaped or left square. Slim timbers can be supported by metal

▽ Generous timbers span an exotic courtyard, while infill screening provides additional shelter over the main path. If needed, discreet downlights could be channelled into the woodwork.

joist bearers, or hangers, fixed to the wall; once treated with preservative, they can be left clean or painted to bring a touch of brightness and to lift the spirits. The hangers, used with other metal elements, such as scaffolding poles, uprights or slim side panels of punched steel, can become part of the overall design.

I know of a very successful structure put together from lengths of recycled timber planks, with slim roofing battens used as rafters for added decoration, all of which were retrieved from skips. The overhead screening spans a corridor space between walls and spreads out, in a modular form, to link across the garden to give the impression that the boundaries are 'holding hands'. The overhead timbers are closely spaced beside the house but are graduallly spaced further apart as the more natural feel of the garden becomes apparent. At the same time they continue to define the spaces for family use – a holistic approach that suits the ecological principles of the owners.

Infill panels of lattice, with battens set square or laid at angles, will give added overhead cover and will work especially well if used selectively, giving extra screening over selected areas so that patches of strong light contrast with areas of dappled shade. Steel rods are suitable as a lighter infill and will integrate well with modern materials. Tactile, shiny metals and a light network of wires, either fixed to vine eyes in the walls or held taut with marine fittings, make a snappy and bright screen and are a good foil for foliage texture without taking up valuable space – a fresh

△ A trellis that is infilled with narrow battens or wires will cast an intricate pattern of shadows on the ground beneath.

▷ Using a trellis infill in alternate sections of an overhead extension will create areas of contrasting shade within a single structure.

and up-to-date flexible style to suit an urban site. Clothe the wires with tendrils of an evergreen honeysuckle and a softer screen will develop.

Different materials and textural combinations can give some relief from what can be over-romanticized associations and bring us right up to date, as long as they are used with sensitivity. Steel is flexible and relatively easy to mould to shape, whether it is used in the form of angular sections or smooth tubular lengths. It can come with a smart lustre, it can be painted and sealed, or it can be left untreated to rust – which is not as unpleasant as it sounds: the mellow, red finish looks really stunning with cedar battens as rafters. Galvanized scaffold poles make sturdy uprights, and they can be buffed up to a shine or painted to contrast with timber overheads. Infill the backcloth with a denser material – panels of sand-blasted or etched glass, for example – to complement the effect. In a restricted area, you will probably need these less bulky materials to make the most of the usable space.

If you would like a chic and up-front feature, where light and reflections can play together, a shiny textured framework, such as stainless steel, would be an ideal base over which a topcoat of Dutchman's pipe (*Aristolochia macrophylla*) could clamber. The handsome, heart-shaped foliage and snaky tendrils would make a snug enclosure, and it has enough personality to make a single statement without supporting climbers. Most metalwork specialists enjoy challenges and will readily give input and advise on using their materials in varied situations.

△ Spaces with personality evolve from individual responses. This tendency is evident here, where the coloured glass panels help to unify the other, rather disparate elements.

Clothing with plants

It is important to be discerning, at least at the start of the process, when choosing the right plants to add to an overhead screen. Simplicity is the guiding rule – it will make the selection process easier and prevent a messy confusion later.

Certain situations demand self-discipline. Overhead screening with a strong architectural style, for example, needs only a single type of climber to supply the soft cover – any fussy grouping would destroy the whole effect. Certain plants also look uncomfortable with companions – their foliage, habit or framework has sufficient character that the plant stands best alone as a major statement, without frills. I have already mentioned Dutchman's pipe (*Aristolochia macrophylla*) in this category; other strong personalities include Chinese gooseberry (*Actinidia deliciosa*), crimson glory vine (*Vitis coignetiae*), the climbing hydrangea (*Hydrangea anomala* subsp. *petiolaris*), which has the bonus of attractive, flaky winter stems, or the somewhat similar but evergreen climbing viburnum (*Pileostegia viburnoides*). The placing of plants is, of course, a highly personal decision, and I prefer to see wisteria used as a single specimen, with nothing to detract from its appeal throughout the year – sculptural stems in winter, elegant foliage that fans in the breeze in summer and an all-too-brief cascade of scented pea-blossoms.

Aspect will have a bearing on your choice of plant. In urban areas, climbers that tolerate pollution are a bonus – climbing ivies (*Hedera* spp.) and virginia creeper (*Parthenocissus quinquefolia*), with *Rosa* 'Madame Alfred Carrière', trumpet vine (*Campsis radicans*) or some varieties of clematis giving a more ornamental effect. For total opulence anywhere choose *Rosa* 'New Dawn' or *R.* 'Albertine' to spread a great quantity of scented blooms voluptuously over any large structure.

Where you need a fast screen, you could consider *Ampelopsis glansulosa* var. *brevipedunculata*, the ornamental and fruiting vines, *Clematis montana* or the evergreen *Clematis armandii* – all will charge off quickly. *Clematis alpina* and *C. macropetala* are also reliable spring flowerers. In a sheltered position common white jasmine (*Jasminum officinale*) and *Lonicera tragophylla* will quickly provide dappled shade overhead. The most showy climber in autumn is Boston ivy (*Parthenocissus tricuspidata*), while yellow-flushed ivies – *Hedera helix* 'Buttercup' and *H. h.* 'Oro di Bogliasco', for example – provide lively year-round colour. They associate well with winter jasmine (*Jasminum nudiflorum*), followed in the summer by confederate jasmine (*Trachelospermum jasminoides*), which I love for its sweetly scented, little starry flowers. For a more delicate effect, the ferny foliage and understated flowers of *Clematis cirrhosa* will provide a soft ceiling to any sheltered open extension.

Most buds reach towards the light before flowering, so the outside surfaces of uprights and overheads are often ablaze with colour, making the screen a focal point from other parts of the garden and leaving the interior a cool, frothy green cocoon. Some climbing plants and wall shrubs, however, have flowers and fruit that hang down and brush your head. For this effect – and remember to allow sufficient overhead clearance – try *Itea ilicifolia*, with pale green racemes that can be 40cm (16in) long, or hybrid vines, which will give you pendulous bunches of fruit.

Look beyond climbers, too. For an early screen, you could consider varieties of the Japanese quince (*Chaenomeles japonica*), which, although not a climber by nature, will thrust upwards with some help. Ceanothus, which comes in evergreen or deciduous species, will happily be trained upwards and give a cloud of fuzzy blue flowers either in spring or autumn – some, such as *Ceanothus* 'A.T. Johnson', flower in both seasons. In a sheltered position Moroccan broom (*Cytisus battandieri*) will spread to form a silvery cloak; its curious yellow flowers look and smell like little pineapples. See the Plant Directory for more detailed information on these and many other plants.

If you decide that a layered look – using plants to prolong the interest through the seasons – suits both you and the setting, check that their habits do not clash. The companion plants need to do well in similar conditions, of course, but also to be well mannered in their behaviour so that they do not smother their neighbours. In addition, you should make sure that you can, for example, clip back the winter jasmine (*Jasminum nudiflorum*) before a summer-flowering clematis scrambles over it or that the vicious character of a spiky plant won't inhibit you from pruning back or tying in its neighbours. For obvious reasons, plants with spiky leaves or thorns are not appropriate for the exposed corners of uprights; instead. try the thornless *Rosa* 'Zéphirine Drouhin', which has a continual display of perfumed blooms in a rich pink colour. There are also certain plants that should be avoided near any busy garden areas – the dust from the stems of *Fremontodendron californicum*, for instance, is an irritant.

▽ Symmetry and a certain formality have been introduced into this town garden. The domed roof over the delicate arbour is reflected in the spherical plant forms. and the curve of the flat paving pattern.

Overhead screening

To encourage lush plants for an overhead screen, there needs to be adequate space and depth of soil in which they can grow, either in a ribbon bed or as squares around the base. Ideally, the planting space needs to be at least 30cm (12in) free from surface paving to take account of foundations and possible rain shadow from the overheads, and this decent width of soil also allows for planting a soft skirt around the base of certain climbers, such as clematis, that need their roots in shade. You will need to hand water and mulch in the early stages to help the climbers get established

Climbers will need a support system suitable for their particular type (see page 50) and the situation; in an exposed position, one breakage can mean damage to the other companion plants. The plants can be tied into lengths of wire fixed with vine eyes or staples along the face of the timber uprights, while metal poles can have eyelet hooks bolted into the casing. The dense base growth of herbaceous climbers can be held with chicken wire neatly wrapped around stout piers.

Ideally, you should begin with a strong base plant, possibly evergreen or one with a muscular framework, like a reasonably vigorous rose, around which to build the picture. If you are worried about having a straggly, bare-looking base, partner it with something like an evergreen honeysuckle, such as *Lonicera japonica* or *L. henryi*, or the evergreen *Ceanothus impressus* to smother the base. By choosing companion plants for their varying flowering and fruiting times and colour combinations you will create an encompassing screen that will provide interest and appeal for much of the year.

Colour preference is very personal. The lime green tone of the golden-leaved hop (*Humulus lupulus* 'Aurea') is not to everyone's taste, and it will look entirely unappealing accompanied by the strong purple of *Clematis* 'The President'. Apply a small colour shift, however, and the yellow canary creeper (*Tropaeolum peregrinum*) wending its way up into the dark blue panicles of *Ceanothus* 'Autumnal Blue' provides an exhilarating contrast. This form of painting with plants is a bit like being let loose in a sweet shop, so here are just a few ideas to whet the appetite. Bear in mind that colour combinations can be categorized into harmonizing and contrasting – harmonies, such as yellow and orange or blue and purple, are adjacent on a colour wheel, while contrasts such as blue and yellow, are opposite – and that contrasts will create a more obvious focal point.

Plant chocolate vine (*Akebia quinata*), with its fragrant, dark brooding flowers in spring, together with the warm, changing tones of *Rosa chinensis* 'Mutabilis' or *R.* 'Phyllis Bide' against a smoky backcloth of the purple-leaved vine, *Vitis vinifera* 'Purpurea'.

Combine the fresh silvery foliage of another ornamental vine, *Vitis vinifera* 'Incana', with the white form of the semi-evergreen potato vine (*Solanum jasminoides* 'Album') – unfortunately not always hardy – and add *Rosa* 'Paul's Perpetual White', which flowers from early summer to late autumn, all to give a ghostly effect against a dark, sheltered background. You could mix in a pale blue clematis, too.

Another rather decadent combination with the same gorgeous *Vitis vinifera* 'Incana' is the extraordinary *Rosa* 'Veilchenblau', whose fragrant blooms come in varying violet and purple tones. Add *Clematis montana* var. *rubens* for early interest, and a honeysuckle – *Lonicera periclymenum* 'Serotina', for example. Both have suitably dark foliage to contrast with the soft, silvery vine leaves. Plant a lower skirt of *Rosa* 'Ferdinand Pichard' to echo the mottled colouring of *R.* 'Veilchenblau'.

4 GARDENS WITHIN A GARDEN

INTRODUCING some discreet divisions within a garden has several advantages. Adding a secondary level of screening means that a double skin forms to enhance the seclusion – boundaries alone are not always high enough to screen adequately or dense enough to soak up noise. Neither are boundaries always suitable as a backcloth to a seating area, especially if they are doing the same job in the same position on your neighbour's side. Alternatively, you might want to increase your sense of privacy, but overhead screening may not be feasible. Areas for relaxing don't have to be snug against boundaries, of course, and dividing a garden can bring new sunny or sheltered areas into use or enable you to enjoy interesting views and features only appreciated from the heart of the garden.

There can be aesthetic reasons for creating separate areas, too, as well as practical ones or psychological necessity. Contradictory though it may at first seem, dividing an open plot can make it appear larger, not smaller, and internal screening is very effective at refocusing your attention. You will also be adding interest with layers of screening material instead of relying on a heavy line around the boundary. The Chinese purposely divided their garden space and crafted gardens for each season and specific parts of the day, with white flowers and bark that would be illuminated by moonlight and groves planted for autumn colour. Their ideas can be adapted to give purpose and personality to our own private spaces.

To divide is not to take away

Gardens are built of space and dividing the space can provide rooms that surprise us and a garden that allows for anticipation and discovery – seeing everything at one glance can be dull. Just as you can give more sense of space to a small area by closing it in, you can give even more feeling of space by then splitting it into compartments that can be visually linked but remain quite separate. By using low walls or hedges to break up the garden into a series of asymmetrical compartments at 45 degrees to one another, you could ensure that the complete garden is never visible as a whole.

The key is to keep divisions simple. You want to make sure that the space remains uncluttered and that you do not create an assault course. Privacy from others in the garden can be planned into the scheme. A children's play area needs to be apart from a dreamy space where a hammock is slung beneath a suitable tree; a sunken court intended for quiet introspection would be better sited away from the main concourse around the backdoor. Even partial screening, either low level or filtered sections of a higher barrier, gives privacy to those using the space as well as allowing those outside to glimpse in and realize that privacy is to be respected. Just one simple panel or a curve of planting is often sufficient, although in extremis you might wish to conceal yourself completely. In a small space this will be difficult to achieve with success without creating a 'cubicle' effect, but a larger garden may lend itself to one or more 'gardens within the garden', initiating a feeling of progress around the garden and providing more opportunity for different degrees of privacy. Secret gardens are the ultimate in privacy, and small individual hideaways are discussed in the next chapter.

◁◁ Beech (*Fagus* spp.) is the traditional material for creating elegant divisions within the garden. Raising one of the arches into a simple curve brings a touch of informality to an otherwise formal scheme.

◁ The timber structure, narrow path and well-proportioned focal point come together to form a vista that has such impact that the adjoining compartments remain relatively secluded.

▷ More than simply a charmingly rustic dividing wall – the sense of privacy that lies beyond is conveyed with the perfect proportions of the arched opening, the attention to detail in the use of the materials and the lack of any obvious focal point.

Building divisions within the garden will underline its three-dimensional aspect, bringing to life the flat pattern of a design on paper. Circles, ovals and curves grow up in planted and constructed bulk to embrace and contain, while right angles and zigzags are useful in providing strong corners that screen. Where entire shapes might be overpowering, parts of a shape – an arc rather than a circle, an angle rather than a completed square – are more successful, being less obtrusive but nevertheless still providing the privacy you seek.

As we noted in Chapter 1, simple geometric shapes work well because they reflect the architectural shape of the buildings in which we live. Squares and rectangles can be used as static shapes in isolation or in formal symmetrical patterns to give a sense of order and rigidity. A strong 'pattern' to your garden will help to concentrate the mind and negate disturbance from the surroundings.

As a form, a circle can give a feeling of containment, harmony and intimacy. Circles are also useful in situations where the eye needs to be distracted away from eyesores in the distance and encouraged inwards and downwards. But beware: because they can be such perfect shapes and private spaces, it can seem a shame to enter them – as though you are breaking a spell. In smaller gardens, the surrounding mass that makes the circular space will need to mask any irregularities in the shape of the site; nothing should jar and interrupt the desired effect. Beware also that, because the circle will compel your eyes down to the lower level, it will compel your neighbours on a higher level to do the same thing, which rather defeats the object. One circular space among other angular forms is often sufficient; used without discretion, the effect is lost.

Triangles and converging or parallel lines will pull the eye in the direction in which they point. Overlapping geometric shapes will provide a sense of movement in the garden, whether they are used diagonally or laid parallel to the house walls. They have the effect of encouraging you onwards, to progress perhaps to a secret area, which is especially useful in a long, rectangular garden.

You could call these tricks or illusions, which of course they are, but they are effective at seemingly pushing your space this way and that, to reduce the impact of negative issues. Shape, form and line can also be used to expand, raise or flatten. Usually, we all crave more room – to have larger parties, for better games of football or to grow more plants – but we frequently have to make do with tricks to create an illusion of space.

A harmonious whole

Garden compartments should link, one to another, to give the whole garden a rhythm, with transient interest through the year. Lifestyles and a growing interest in holistic ideologies tell us that these compartments should not be enclosed in manicured, fussy boxes but instead should subtly serve to develop sheltered areas and adjust, as nature does, to the seasons. An internal screen may be an all-encompassing evergreen hedge or it may be no more than a suggestion – an arc of lavender to define a 'dining area' or a stand of giant grass to shield a small scented garden without obscuring a view.

As you divide the garden to create extra layers of privacy, it is necessary to consider how these areas will link together, how you travel through on foot or with your eye. These links are very important as they are the tools that give unity to the garden as a whole and provide just

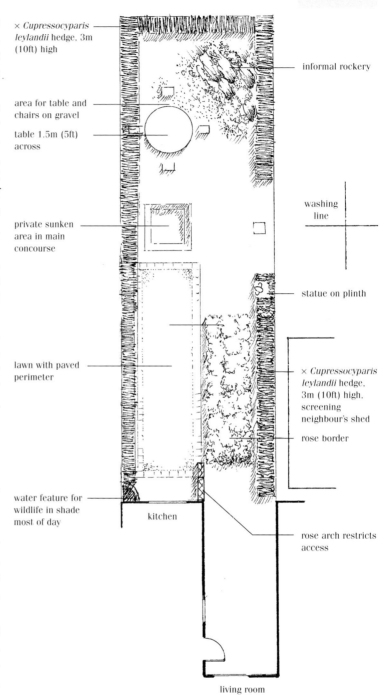

x *Cupressocyparis leylandii* hedge, 3m (10ft) high

informal rockery

area for table and chairs on gravel

table 1.5m (5ft) across

washing line

private sunken area in main concourse

statue on plinth

x *Cupressocyparis leylandii* hedge, 3m (10ft) high, screening neighbour's shed

rose border

lawn with paved perimeter

water feature for wildlife in shade most of day

kitchen

rose arch restricts access

living room

△ This garden plan illustrates perfectly an unhappy and unwise division of the long, narrow shape. The garden appears even more elongated than it is because of the tall, blanket screening and the narrow lawn, which becomes a muddy corridor in wet weather. From the kitchen the view is of the sitting area; from the living room the view is across the roses – unattractive for half the year – to the rockery and, beyond, to the hedge. The sitting area is made awkward by its proximity to the rockery.

a hint of what lies beyond. The light and shade cast by enclosing elements contribute to the dynamics and the atmosphere of the whole garden – dappled shade across the main terrace will emphasize the contrast of the full evening sun over a smaller, more intimate space; a rhythm of forms repeated through the divisions will help knit and harmonize. This can be achieved with simple repetition of a paving detail, specimen plant or the use of hedging of the same species.

As we move away from the house, areas should become less geometric, more irregular; circles and curves, rarely successful near the house, can break through the straight lines. A well-balanced relationship between the formality and informality of the different areas will still need to be maintained, but large spaces can embrace smaller ones and unfold into satisfying shapes and compartments with their own kind of furnishing.

Movement through different areas can be dictated by the choice of floor surface – soft grass and gravel, for example, will force a slower pace than textured paving with a good grip. A change of surface, such as a rectangle of cobblestones in a wide gravel path, can identify a change of direction. Planting can also compel one to linger at certain points – aromatic foliage begging to be brushed with the hand or tall yew hedging encompassing a simple grassed circle, where movement is arrested and the eye drawn up towards the sky. A contemplative space.

▷ A curved path, snug in baby's tears (*Soleirolia soleirolii*), leads enticingly between borders of predominantly evergreen planting. This is surely a place to linger, where muted tones establish a calm atmosphere.

Internal dividers

Divisions constructed from brick, stone, wood or metal will provide a more instant result and can often add a greater strength to the overall design, while plants as screens will give a softer effect; they will be more tactile and can provide seasonal highlights with perfume, flowers and colour changes. Many of the suggestions for boundaries can make excellent internal divisions; in fact, subtly repeating the same material will contribute to the overall integrated look of the garden. But with comfort and subtle enclosure rather than security and complete privacy in mind, the possibilities broaden.

Walls

In small gardens, where space is at a premium, solid walls as dividers could be inappropriate; even a single brick wall has a thickness that is inappropriate where conditions are cramped. Where space permits, however, walls are comforting and enclosing, and internal walls can be more imaginative than a boundary wall may allow. Carefully angled or built to form a corner, they are ideal double-sided sun-traps. Brick walls are strong enough to support overhead beams, and seating, ledges and barbecues can be extended outwards to give a smooth, uncluttered appearance to an outdoor eating area. Walls built with a honeycomb structure and rendered or simply painted in clear, strong colours will define an area, provide a screen and still allow the light or the land beyond to complete the picture. Free-standing walls can easily be designed with openings for viewing or progressing through.

Walling materials, whether stone, brick, slate or flint, present a naturally decorative surface, or they can provide a flat vertical face for a layer of ceramic, mosaic, shells, or they can be roughly stuccoed or painted. A water wall will crave attention, the sparkling sheet of water rippling over its surface immediately diverting eye and ear away from any less pleasant elements in the surroundings. Walls are worth every penny.

Hurdles and woven fences

Even small fences can have a presence, and without additional planting they can underline a static, peaceful atmosphere, with the emphasis placed on horizontal lines, or they can be repeated to enhance a feeling of movement. Hurdles woven from coppiced hazel make adaptable rustic-style panels that provide shelter from wind; they will stand strong and straight if fixed to hardwood stakes of oak or chestnut. Hazel and willow rods can also be bent and joined to create less traditional flat or three-dimensional forms that suit both small and large gardens.

Old garden, new garden

Walled gardens from older, more lavish eras still have an element of contained surprise, almost like opening a box of chocolates.

Originally, walled gardens were often sited well away from the main house, beyond the formal gardens and close to the landscape. Today, they make ideal leisure areas, being sheltered and screened, and a rectangular swimming pool fits very well into the architectural framework. The contrast of modern leisure within and wild flower meadows or orchard without is enchanting.

Windows can be punctured into the walls to capture views; sides can be replaced with glass sheets to maintain shelter but increase the light, and sun-facing sides can be reduced in height or removed completely. Food and play seem to go hand in hand, and whatever the proposed use for the space the porous nature of the brickwork ensures a comforting warmth that still remains an ideal surface for espaliered or fan-trained fruit.

In the medieval monastic *jardin clos*, branches were woven into fences to enclose raised beds; drawing inspiration from representations of biblical gardens, the makers often used chestnut branches. The world today is a very different place from when medieval gardens were governed by strict rules of enclosure and segregation, but the idea is not redundant. Pliable young withies can be woven into panels that will sprout leaves in spring to make a whimsical screen.

MAINTAINING HARMONY IN A SUB-DIVIDED GARDEN

SEPARATE parts of a garden can have quite different personalities and still remain in harmony with each other. Where the division is fragmented or filtered – in other words, where it is not a solid screen – a simple repetition of shape, texture, material or colour will be enough to ensure that the overall unity is maintained.

In this rectangular garden, delicate wafts of colour are used sparingly but successfully to maintain a rhythm from one area to the other. Yellow achilleas in the nearest enclosure are echoed in the sunny tones in the background; the deep mauves and pinks of violas and foxgloves are mirrored in the foliage of spiky, dark red cordylines – and even when the espaliered fruit can in time form a screen without the supporting canes, a hint of what lies beyond will still be part of the charm in this garden.

In the foreground the well-defined borders reflect the proximity of the house just behind the camera lens. These are packed with structural evergreen planting, which provides an underlying shape to the glorious summer flowers that bloom with abandon, well sheltered by the yew hedge on the left. Through the rose arch the drop in level towards the end of the

plot has been used imaginatively to reinforce the change in atmosphere into the informal garden where the relaxed planting style marries well with the rusticity of the garden building.

The balance will shift with the seasons, the decorative quality of the formal garden in spring and summer giving way to the two strong elements of the garden house and the pool, which will take on the role of major features through autumn and winter. A heavier screen would not have allowed such an appreciation of this well co-ordinated and highly effective division of a garden space.

◁ A double barrier is formed from materials with similarly graceful forms. The one that is alive and understandably more adventurous, Amur silver grass (*Miscanthus sacchariflorus*), is held firmly in place by woven bamboo staves.

Bamboo

Cut bamboo used as a screen can be treated in a more architectural fashion, with the sections framed, holding crossbars and canes for durability. These panels look good painted with strong, contrasting colours: black and white are ideal. Water, mirrors, pebbles and evergreen structural plants associate very well with this look.

Variations on the theme include Japanese bamboo sleeve fences, with their single sloping side like a kimono sleeve, and panels of diamond lattice bamboo finished with a binding of brushwood along the top and bottom. An oriental look can also be achieved by a sandwich of vertical timber battens encasing sheets of a fine geotextile in a natural, stony colour. Strong and resistant to tearing, this looks good applied to another surface as an inner skin. Used with the light behind it, it takes on the look of tough paper, but as a free-standing screen it would need to be in a very sheltered position.

Trellising

Trellis gives immediate height with relatively minimal thickness and is, therefore, a very useful medium for secondary screening. Hardwood trellis from sustainable sources will be costly, but it is very durable and, if not treated, will mature to a silvery grey. Treated softwood with a sawn finish takes any stain well. It can be stained to merge gently into the background so that associated planting steals the limelight, or it can be an architectural statement in its own right. Trellis is available in a variety of sizes and styles, but a contemporary style that reflects the strength of the associated building will be more satisfactory in the long term than pseudo-traditional trellis panels with incorrect scale, arched tops and finials, a style that suits very few situations.

Finely knit lattice, whether in square or diamond pattern, gives almost complete privacy and, if constructed with the slats notched together, the surface will be flush. Where trellis is backed by a mirror it will reflect light and glimpses of neighbouring areas as well as create an illusion of space and an indefinable sense of 'transparent enclosure'.

Glass and metal

Strengthened glass screens, used as dividers, reflect and brighten a dull corner when the sun's rays hit the surface. They don't glare and have an added bonus of becoming transparent when the sun or an artificial light source glows from behind. Panels of coloured reinforced glass have the same attributes but can also form blocks of striking colour to mask and define silhouettes in a playful scheme.

Metals are an underused material, especially in a structural context in outdoor areas, although they are flexible, easy to construct and fix, inexpensive and also stylish. Where the metal is coated – plastic-coated chain-link with a black or dark coloured finish, for example – it can be used as a short-term fence until encroaching planting grows and fills out. In the same way as they make contemporary

▽ The soft grey-blue stain on the risers and most of the decking merges gently into the foliage, while touches of stronger blues appear in odd lengths of the decking. The colours are repeated in the railing and house exterior. The stronger blue makes the hammock a focus of the scene, with the soft grey-green of the foliage and a blue Atlantic cedar providing the harmony.

Unifying with colour

Colour often succeeds in bringing mongrel elements in a composition together. Containers, gates, trellis and furniture can be finished with the same or similar tones to help unite different areas of the garden. The sunny colours, ranging from lime green through yellow, orange, terracotta and reds to purple, tend to be attention-seekers and will certainly attract interest. The middle colours in this range, orange and red, appear to leap forward and so foreshorten the space. Dark colours, which provide stability and give weight to objects, are especially useful as a base 'skirt', causing white and pale tones above them to appear to float.

1 *Cedrus libani* subsp. *atlantica* Glauca Group

2 *Athyrium niponicum*

3 *Hydrangea arborescens* 'Grandiflora'

4 *Philadelphus coronarius* 'Variegatus'

uprights for overhead screening (see page 57), sleek metal poles holding tensioned steel wires are the very lightest of structures and create an elegant, filigree effect with gentle climbers to cast some shade below. A row of aluminium twist supports clothed in runner beans make an effective light summer screen where you do not wish to be deprived of the view beyond.

Hedging

Hedging can grow into a more intimate screen that is decorative and attractive and lends itself to changes in height, flowing curves or regimented castellations. A staggered screen running through the garden, with gaps for access, will lead on invitingly. It is also very adaptable – a springy plant such as box (*Buxus sempervirens*), for example, can be support or reinforcement, a method of containing or a feature in its own right, providing a restful landscape without flowers.

Internal hedges are an opportunity to emphasize and tie in boundary hedging, perhaps on a smaller scale – a slender thread of dark yew or holly under a light line of rowans and crab apples might pick up the more solid mass of a yew or holly boundary hedge.

△ Fragrant jasmine (*Jasminum officinale*) twines through a simple square trellis to create a partial screen. The inset stained glass panel provides a delicate contrast.

▷ Low divisions can be composed of hedges and edges of varying heights that do not gobble up precious space. Here cordon fruit is sandwiched between aromatic plants and hedges of box (*Buxus* spp.).

▷ Layers of plants, from the carpet of grass to the canopy of spring blossom, form textural partitions. The crinkly brown autumn foliage of both beech (*Fagus* spp.) and hornbeam (*Carpinus* spp.) can still be seen in sheltered places.

Using single species hedging for internal divisions gives a sense of formality or can provide a symmetry without being formal in character. Staggered lines of beech (*Fagus sylvatica*) forming lighter colonnades or as simple raised screens would complement the rectangular shape of a formal pool; water and beech are a wonderful combination.

Of course, it takes time to clip neat, sharp lines or box or yew, which must be done at least two or three times a year, but there are many small shrubs that create charming small hedges. Evocatively scented lavender (*Lavandula* spp.) needs clipping down only after flowering, as does rosemary (*Rosmarinus officinalis*), which would form a tough, aromatic hedge near the house or around a barbecue area. Silky *Artemisia arborescens* would give a low silver barrier, or try the neat form of cotton lavender, *Santolina pinnata* subsp. *neopolitana*, aromatic again and with the bonus of tight buttons of lemon yellow flowers in summer. An evergreen with a deeper tone, sweet box (*Sarcococca hookeriana* var. *humilis*), provides a honeyed winter scent that draws you to it on bright, sunny winter days and retains its neat, glossy foliage to balance more showy summer performers. The evergreen forms of berberis make good dividers: they are very tolerant and you can clip them tightly or let them arch. *Berberis darwinii* makes a splendid show of small, shiny leaves on fanning branches with vibrant orange flowers in spring, and B. × *hybridogagnepainii* 'Chenaultii' has pendulous double flowers in a softer, citrus yellow.

Trees as definers

Slender tree stems can mark divisions in a small space. The smaller species of rowan (*Sorbus cashmiriana* and *S. vilmorinii*) have delicate habits, autumn fruits and foliage colour and will provide an ornamental, filigree screen. In a larger garden, flowering crabs (*Malus hupehensis*, *M.* × *schiedeckeri* 'Hillieri' and *M.* 'Evereste') and the mop-headed acacia (*Robinia pseudoacacia* 'Umbraculifera') will give similar effects when planted in a single or double line to create an intimate aisle.

Ballerina and Minarette apples form narrow spires that, when grown in a row, will form a decorative and productive screen. Other fruit trees on dwarfing rootstocks can be trained as a row of cordons at an angle of 45 degrees or pruned into fan or espalier shapes.

Pleaching – the training of branches to provide horizontal and vertical screens – gives a less dense screen than tall hedging, which can have a deadening effect. Slender trees can form single avenues in medium-sized gardens, and in larger ones they can be used to define axes and routes or to make avenues, allowing glimpses through under the canopy and letting the line of trunks lightly show the way.

△ The structural framework of espaliered fruit trees makes a striking statement before the foliage unfolds.

◁ Even plants that have been forcibly trained – such as these pleached lime trees (*Tilia* spp.) – develop their own characteristic patterns of growth.

A row of standard holly clipped into pyramids or more fanciful topiary – a variegated form will give a quite different impression from the more sombre green – or thin pencils of Irish yew (*Taxus baccata* 'Fastigiata') make impressive dividers and will certainly be noticed.

Living tunnels

In larger gardens, pergolas and tunnels of shrubs can provide an internal screen while at the same time encouraging us to move about the garden. If they are to work successfully, such structures need to be carefully placed or they will simply become another awkward feature that doesn't quite fit and isn't used. A pergola clothed in climbers can be devised either for year-round greenery or with the intention that each autumn the foliage should fall away to reveal a skeletal but still beautiful structure. Using the plant combinations suggested for overhead screening in Chapter 3, you could create a living feature that provides the seclusion of a hedge but also contributes a long succession of colour from flowers or fruit and has an added 'secret passage' element. Remember to allow sufficient space for the plants' growth; as they fill out they will narrow and lower the overall dimensions considerably.

Living tunnels are markedly less common in our gardens than the ubiquitous pergola, but they create more structure with more personality. The classic yew tunnel will be completely private all year, but you will really be planting for posterity as it will be decades before an acceptable result is achieved. Deciduous plants, such as beech (*Fagus* spp.), hornbeam (*Carpinus betulus*), lime (*Tilia* spp.) or willow rods, will give a faster screen but not complete privacy all year. A framework of metal hoops will help add visual weight to deciduous tunnels during the winter.

Planting

Borders have many of the same properties as hedging and can provide greater privacy at different times, although they require more space to be effective. They are a more informal way of dividing the garden space into functional areas, and in Chapter 5 they will be used to contain very private places, that are more poetic than functional. Single-colour planting is also one way to reinforce a sense of a separate area. Island beds are isolated and do not retain space, but borders have a geometry and relationship to other garden components – they have a purpose. The basic ingredients for success are the correct balance and mix of texture, form and habit, with colour added as the final element. Structure counts above all else.

Even with evergreen planting, nothing is static, as new growth causes changes in the spread as well as the height. The greatest change, however, will occur during the seasons with the growth pattern of perennials and change in structure of deciduous shrubs. Think how the development into leaf of elder (*Sambucus* spp.), *Hydrangea aspera*, Japanese angelica tree (*Aralia elata*) and meadow rue (*Thalictrum* spp.) changes the appearance and bulk of the plant, which then changes again as autumn turns to winter. If borders are to have a specific screening role during winter as well as summer, the percentage of deciduous planting should be relatively low. The higher the percentage used, the greater the change in the look of the planting mass.

◁◁ A formal arrangement of trees – these are lime trees (*Tilia* spp.) – can appear as a tunnel from one angle and also be used to imply division from another aspect, from where the apparently single line of trunks will appear as a rhythmic barrier beneath the continuous canopy.

A SUNKEN GARDEN

THE changes in level that form a sunken garden should always be fluid and gentle – after all, you are creating an inviting saucer or court, not a pit. A contrast in material can contribute to the effect – stone steps, for example, leading down from gravel or paving to a soft, aromatic rug of camomile or thyme. Alternatively, you could process down from a lawn by way of simple paving into a sunken gravel garden theaded with libertias, low, tufty sedges and ground-hugging sedums, given pzzazz with a summer dusting of bright Californian poppies (*Eschscholzia californica*). Grass steps are wonderfully

Plan of a sunken garden

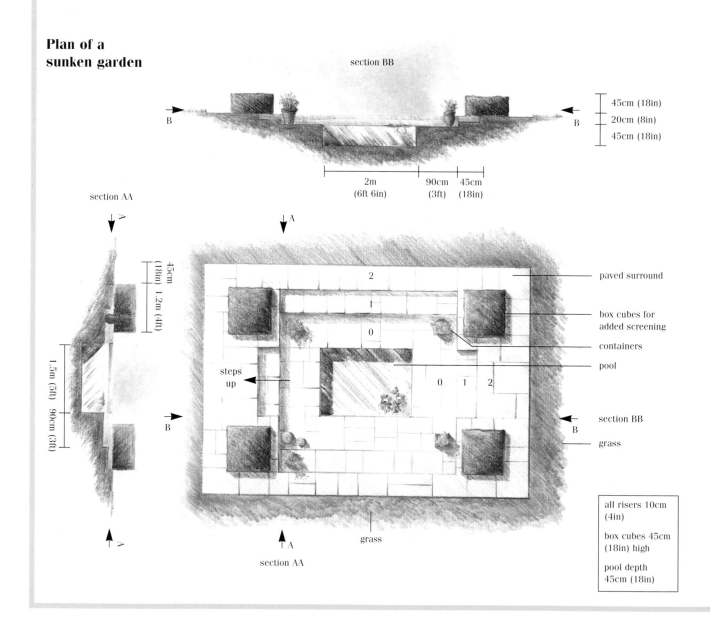

section BB

45cm (18in)
20cm (8in)
45cm (18in)

2m (6ft 6in)
90cm (3ft)
45cm (18in)

section AA

45cm (18in)
1.2m (4ft)

1.5m (5ft)
90cm (3ft)

2

1

0

steps up

0 1 2

B

B

paved surround

box cubes for added screening

containers

pool

section BB

grass

grass

section AA

all risers 10cm (4in)

box cubes 45cm (18in) high

pool depth 45cm (18in)

elegant but need space to be shown off to their full potential, and the angle of the slope and the depth of the tread will need careful working out, both to look right visually and to avoid making mowing unnecessarily difficult (check the width and weight of your mower at the planning stage).

This simple geometric plan can serve as a template for many styles. Size, shape and planting can be adjusted as you please, but the proportions are a useful guide to achieving a sunken area that is neither too fussy and cramped nor so loose that its sense of envelopment is lost. Risers of about 10cm (4in) give a comfortable graduation, while perimeter planting – here, box (*Buxus* spp.) clipped into 45cm (18in) cubes – gives extra, tactile screening and increases the sunken effect without adding to the excavation work. For obvious safety reasons, there needs to be sufficient space immediately around the little carpet of water, especially as the steps are perfect for lolling about on.

Planted containers at the corners will emphasize the enclosed atmosphere and also soften the angles if necessary – lily-flowered tulips, lilies and agapanthus would make a perfect succession of planting by the water. Reduced to fit a very compact setting, the pool could be replaced by a group of shallow bowls holding water or low-planted containers – all to attract the attention and concentrate the mind.

The corner of a small sunken area

Positioning the plants is largely a matter of personal choice, but it would make sense to avoid placing plants with thorns and spikes near the edging paths and seating areas. Loose, informal planting will have a quite unrestricted feeling, allowing the habit of the plants to show freely, with the additional highlight of changes in tones and bright spots of colour adding to the overall tapestry.

Changes in level

All the effects considered so far have been to provide screening above ground, but you can also achieve a sense of seclusion by dropping down into the garden. Nothing creates interest in a garden more than breaking up a continuous surface; even slight changes of level make all the difference, bringing interest and emphasis to sweeps of planting and a change in atmosphere. Even if just one area of planting can be raised to break the flatness, it will lift the interest of the whole garden.

Where you have space, you can afford to allow the shaping to be subtle – low sunken walls, gentle slopes, wide banks and shallow, broad steps will all impose a leisurely pace and ambience throughout the garden. In a small garden any change in level will be a positive arrangement of steps and terraces, and on a steep gradient you will need to incorporate retaining walls to hold the soil in place. These might become a major feature or be disguised with heavy planting.

Ground shaping needs to be carried out with panache; make sweeps not pimples and ridges. This will demand adequate space for good sweeps of contouring. Contours should echo an existing line or curve, which might be an established planting area or a snake of water – a gentler effect is achieved by letting the line of the curve fade out gradually, instead of finishing it with a hard end.

Planting on terrace faces or on the slopes of contours will need bulk and substance. It won't necessarily be high, but it should be dense, not wispy. Thick rims of lavender or osmanthus or flowing sweeps of ivy, all planted through netting secured to the ground, will mask the angles created by land forming. Planted slopes will provide a contrast with the finer texture of grass, and low, ground-hugging plants will give you a soft mattress to lie back on.

Outdoor living rooms

One of the advantages of sub-dividing a garden is that, like our interior living space, we can create different areas for different functions or moods. You could end up with several different 'rooms' within a garden, each private from the rest as well as from the outside world. Each area needs to serve its purpose, have a personality and still fit in with the overall harmony.

Probably the most popular 'room' is one for eating out and entertaining in fine weather. Many of the practicalities of creating an outside dining area were looked at in Chapter 3 (see page 47), but if your boundary provides sufficient privacy you may not feel the need to roof in your eating area. Containers will reinforce the entrance to the 'room' as well as signal any change in level. Any planting in these pots or adjacent to them needs to be inviting and assured with a certain formality: avoid the unkempt look. Inside, more containers could continue the theme or a more informal look could take over; whichever option you choose, aromatic foliage and scented flowers will contribute to a relaxed atmosphere.

Just one length of extra screening may be enough to designate this as a separate area – a row of containers, a compact hedge or a low wall (which will also provide useful perching points) can give a contained feeling while allowing you to enjoy a view into the rest of the garden.

▷ Using evergreen shrubs and small trees in containers to divide space is often a necessary but successful strategy in small gardens. Strength of form, shape and habit are essential.

Privacy at play

Swimming pools and tennis courts are a mixed blessing: on a warm summer's day their benefits are obvious, but they do raise particular problems for privacy. Swimming pools, in particular, should be sheltered – but not by trees that will fill them with leaves every autumn – and allow you to feel sufficiently private to lounge around in comfort. Viewed from the outside, a hard tennis court seldom adds beauty to a garden, and in climates where use is limited and pool covers are a necessity, there is no more depressing and unnecessary sight than a swimming pool put under wraps but left open to view. So screening here has a dual function.

Rendered concrete block walling, finished with modernistic angles and strong, positive tones enhances a dramatic and stylish pool area; neat brickwork, traditional trellis or fencing has a more classical effect. Add extra interest with trained, espaliered or pleached light trees and underplanting to provide a layered screen. Planting to screen leisure pools should fit the setting and be reasonably tough in habit. Species with thorns and berries should be avoided, and consider the amount of leaf drop that deciduous plants will make – a larger percentage of a soft barrier must be evergreen. Silver and grey foliage plants will contribute to a Mediterranean-style pool area. Tall bamboos work well as a screen for pools near informal, contemporary architecture, associate well with water and give a light, filtered barrier.

If timber vernacular buildings and screens form part of the enclosed space around a pool, a different treatment and atmosphere will evolve. Instead of bamboos, soaring golden oats (*Stipa gigantea*) or pampas grass (*Cortaderia selloana* 'Pumila') provide a rather strange but successful infiltration of meadow or prairie and give watery reflections. Your screening elements can be personalities in their own right.

Solid blocks of hedging around tennis courts only emphasize the awkward shape, but a surround of a well-proportioned pergola or a slim avenue of pleached trees will incorporate a court discreetly into the overall pattern. Green netting should be avoided at all costs because it clamours for attention. Use a plain, grey, galvanized netting or, better still, black plastic-coated netting, which will merge into the background. Where space is not a problem, you may prefer the option of sinking the court below surface level and using the removed earth to contour the surrounding area. Planting across these raised banks will lose the effect of the court in its surroundings.

Children's play areas

A play area for small children will be close to the house, for safety and for practical reasons. As they grow, children need more freedom and more room for expression, and play areas can be created – by you or them – deeper into the garden. Children's play areas and equipment will have a relatively short life span, so it makes good sense, when planning the size, position and the method of screening, to keep to a simple framework that could be developed later – perhaps low hedging (without thorns, for obvious reasons), which will allow a view into the space when children are small and more vulnerable.

▷ Associated planting would help to integrate this vibrant children's play area into the rest of the garden. Very young children at play need to be visible at all times for safety's sake, so dense barriers are unsuitable.

Close access to nature should be a part of childhood. Dens and playhouses, where children's activities are allowed to develop naturally, should be versatile and flexible, to account for daily change in fun and games. They need to be strong, resilient and as indestructible as possible. Bamboo tunnels and rustling rooms, secret dens formed with willow or hazel plaited columns, climbing frames and simple barricades of chestnut poles, even just a simple group of birch trees, will provide a base and 'home' for children. It's important to involve them in the planning. I know a situation where a timber fort was built for the children, in secret as a Christmas present. It was carefully thought out and well-placed, but to their parents' chagrin, the children much preferred the old garden shed near the house.

Timber climbing frames can be remodelled later into an overhead structure and perhaps linked into the boundary, not necessarily with the same material but perhaps with a line of planting or a couple of trees to visually link the whole together.

Screening of utilities

However private, a quiet spot you have created for yourself is not enhanced by a clear view of dustbins or the oil tank, so internal screening should include the masking of unattractive necessities like these.

Storage for compost and garden equipment will need to be contained, but access to and around this area has to be practical and allow for the manipulation of unwieldy wheelbarrows, mowers and other paraphernalia. Practically sited near the main area of garden work, a shady corner will suffice if well screened and covered with a variegated ivy or similarly tough evergreen climber. If sited against the boundary, oil tanks, bins and other utility areas can be enclosed, leaving sufficient access, in the same fabric as the boundary, which will cause them to disappear into the background.

5 OASES AND HAVENS

△ Not exactly a summerhouse and not exactly a tent, but rather a flexible arrangement to withdraw into when life is too much. The cordylines (*Cordyline australis*) in the foreground underline its exotic air.

◁◁ An unassuming arbour forms the entrance to a retreat that is bounded entirely with plants. Scented roses scramble upwards to cover the entrance.

A PRIVATE area where you find true peace and quiet to mull over an idea or just read a newspaper is attainable in most gardens, irrespective of their size and situation. This will be a very personal place, which can be tucked away out of sight or be made into a feature in its own right; it can be sheltered by tree canopies or be out in the open, surrounded by a gentle wave of plants; it could be hidden above eye level or be a sunken dish in the ground. You might seek to recreate a childhood memory or just acquire what you have always wanted. These are intimate places that you might wish to share – or not. They might be snug, but they are certainly not rigid and uncomfortable – you will feel completely at home there in your sheltered retreat from the outside world.

Small garden buildings such as gazebos, pavilions and summerhouses make attractive private sanctums and have the added appeal of roofed-in cosiness. Bowers and arbours – rustic nooks with romantic connotations – have always been places used for assignations, creating the illusion of being in nature although they are close to the house. The foliage overhead will create soothing sounds as well. Smaller secluded arches and private places to sit will counterbalance larger features, and their intimacy should be exploited in the positioning and accompanying planting. With planting alone you can give your oasis a sense of place by using combinations to achieve varying atmospheres, with curving borders, informal sweeps, comforting spreads and, always, gentle protection – plants to provide, more than anything, a special place with an intrinsic charm of its own. All these private places should be few and far between – small elements in small doses.

Gazebos and summerhouses

Whimsical garden houses originated in Persian gardens. They were temporarily or permanently enclosed, according to requirements. In the Middle Ages Crusaders returning from the East brought back with them the oriental custom of using colourful little tents as shelters during the summer months. These were small built frameworks covered with canvas or curtaining and allowed to billow out or tightly looped back. Tents, marquees and ornamental pavilions can be made by commercial tent-makers out of a weatherproof base fabric, over which you can drape or attach a lighter material, tied back on as many sides as you wish, depending on the size of your garden and the privacy you require. Run the necessary utilities up as close as possible or rely on candles, oil lamps and battery power for you to work happily away on your lap-top computer in complete isolation.

More permanent structures, gazebos and pavilions were originally small buildings that overlooked enclosed gardens. They were sheltered resting points that provided privacy but were designed to give a sense of what lay outside – perfume, sound, movement and sheltered enjoyment of the elements.

The modern gazebo unfortunately often ends up as a receptacle for garden furniture instead of being a focus in the overall plan of the garden. To guard against this fate, it should be placed where you can linger, protected from the weather, and enjoy a special scene or the scents and aromas from nearby plants. Make it the centre of a small private space, give it a sense of place and a reason for being and you will use it far more.

All manner of styles for summerhouses have evolved, from kiosks with mosque-like roofs and complicated fretwork to model American colonial pavilions, with simulated tiled roofs and low trelliswork sides. Little buildings with thick fringes of thatch on their conical roofs have a Victorian or Edwardian flavour – they evoke images of the sound of mallet knocking croquet ball and peals of laughter – but they can fit equally well in contrasting settings such as small, woody copses.

A summerhouse on a turntable is probably the ultimate way of ensuring privacy. Such a structure will enable you to turn your back on whatever you want as well as follow the sun from one side of the sky to the other. However, such summerhouses will require more space than the traditional style and may need specialist installation.

▽ Position and treatment go hand in hand. A quirky construction, suitably embellished, will get all the attention it deserves, especially when sited centre stage with a green backdrop as the supporting cast.

In Japan tea houses provide retreats from everyday life, and the ceremonial and philosophical are combined in nourishment and meditation. Specific, easily recognizable garden elements are developed to give a necessary supporting role – stepping stones as a pathway, the stone lantern to light the path, the stone basin to hold water for washing hands – all making a complete small world within a larger garden. In this context it is especially important that the building does not jar with the surroundings, even if the building itself has a role as a feature. Think about developing a special route to make it more mysterious or perhaps emphasizing the path and adjacent planting to make it more obvious.

My favourite summerhouse looks as if it had landed like a translucent shuttlecock in a glade of native trees. A timber and aluminium frame holds glass panels that form the ceiling, sides and doors to give you views in whichever direction you wish. It sparkles as the sun shoots through the overhead foliage but still neatly wraps whoever is inside in a warm, leafy oasis. This beautiful piece of contemporary design contrasts with the surroundings – it does not jar with them.

You can, of course, buy a custom-made gazebo, but a more economical and undoubtedly more enjoyable approach is to put together your own. An old summerhouse or redundant garden shed can be adapted and reshaped to take on a new persona. Play on the aged look with a 'distressed' finish – a coat of milky wash using an eggshell paint or a stain with a soft grey base, such as lichen or powder blue. Add trellis panels stained a darker tone to

◁◁ Building a refuge over water offers the possibility of complete isolation by pulling up a drawbridge. An oriental-style arbour in surroundings such as this may be impracticable in a small garden, but raising a retreat from the ground is a possible solution in the search for privacy.

△ The scale of this summerhouse is correct for its setting among mature trees and tall hedging. By next season the coat of climbing plants will have helped to make it appear in complete harmony with the surrounding planting.

◁ Almost formal and certainly traditional, this little building tucked away in the corner of the plot is well used. The surrounding area is enlivened with fresh summer plantings of sunny nasturtiums and zonal pelargoniums.

make a second skin and extend well-supported side panels like fins to bear climbing plants and to provide a backcloth for tubs and containers. If you wish, carry on adding embellishments in the form of finials and even gargoyles, and then come down to earth with practical paving slabs or decking for flooring and a comfortable seat. Fill tubs with sweet-smelling dianthus or lilies and you'll find you've made a haven.

To help a gazebo or summerhouse sit well in its surroundings, consider the colour and finish of the building in relation to the adjacent planting – a pinky terracotta gazebo set in clouds of the smoke tree (*Cotinus coggygria*), a stronger toned variety for preference, such as *Cotinus* 'Flame' or *C.* 'Grace', or a rustic timber building finished with a very dark stain to contrast with a sea of white poplar (*Populus alba*) or silvery willows, such as white willow (*Salix alba* var. *sericea*) or coyote willow (*S. exigua*). Place a simple summerhouse symmetrically between two or four of the shapely, large-leaved whitebeam, *Sorbus thibetica* 'John Mitchell' (syn. *S. aria* 'Mitchellii'), or in a grove of pollarded eucalyptus as an evergreen cloak – but keep those loppers handy. If you wish to remain unseen, plant a surround of dark elder (*Sambucus nigra* 'Guincho Purple') and the almost black hollyhock, *Alcea rosea* 'Nigra'. Alternatively, you could choose to enclose yourself inside your sanctuary (with a machete) within a thicket of black bamboo (*Phyllostachys nigra*).

Dark green tones for garden buildings are fashionable and very safe. Brighten up the image with a froth of lime green – golden acacia (*Robinia pseudoacacia* 'Frisia') or *Gleditsia triacanthos* 'Sunburst'. In a built-up area, the pollution-tolerant maidenhair tree (*Ginkgo biloba*) would provide another fresh green but quirky ambience, with its fluttery, fan-shaped leaves. Dark green would also be a good foil to delicate, variegated foliage, such as that of *Acer negundo* 'Variegatum'.

Arbours and arches

Probably the lightest but cosiest screening will come from arbours and arches set well back into planted areas – islands within the garden. These small shelters can have varied personalities, ranging from a simple framework smothered in planting in a small, formal town garden, to marble columns with a canopy of vines to suit a large, classically styled garden.

Whether they are positioned to look out on a view or neatly tucked back into a planted area, an intimate hideaway needs be placed where you can be certain of privacy – but good access and the promise of comfort will encourage you to use it, and no matter how small it is, it should have an atmosphere of its own. Arrange the seating to face a pleasant aspect and allow adequate elbow room; the space must be enveloping but still functional – doll's house scale is not right. A little paving or gravel to prevent a muddy floor and fragrant plants on all sides will complete the welcome.

Timber has natural assets that fit well with the intimate character of these private places; the texture is apparent and the material seems to be alive. A wooden frame, with infilled trellis and a handy built-in bench, can be compact enough to fit the smallest plot. Add a curved arch to cover and give shelter, and some moments of privacy are ensured.

Rustic larch poles, fixed and braced, are fine in a rural setting and can support climbers with a lighter constitution. On an informal arbour like this *Clematis alpina* subsp. *sibirica* 'White Moth' followed by *Rosa* 'Maigold' or *R.* 'Leverkusen' and, for late-summer interest, *Clematis orientalis* would give a soft milk-and-butter haze from mid-spring throughout the autumn. Cap it with an open, conical roof to give sensible headroom, and give yourself a simple bench beneath, which will become gently shrouded with the starry white flowers of *Clematis recta*, whose lax stems will ramble at will around your shoulders and under your feet.

▽ The boldly painted arch is accompanied by suitably bold planting – tiger lilies (*Lilium lancifolium*), Dahlia 'Bishop of Llandaff', coreopsis, crocosmia, fennel and ornamental grasses.

Metal can be formed to make a small arbour or arch to your own specification that will undoubtedly be more pleasing than off-the-shelf elements with black nylon coating and clumsy joints. Aluminium, anodized for a smooth, coloured finish, or lengths of mild steel that have the appearance of wrought iron can be welded together to your requirements.

Doubling function with pleasure by forming a resting place surrounded by ripening fruit sounds idyllic. Apple and pear trees can be suitably trained over metal arches and made to wrap around any quiet space, giving sufficient shelter during warm days. The strong skeleton of the trees will be smothered with blossom, foliage and fruit through the seasons. Other decorative trees that lend themselves to similar treatment are the whitebeam, *Sorbus aria* 'Lutescens', which has brilliant silver foliage, or the slow-growing Judas tree (*Cercis siliquastrum*), whose stems and even the trunk are covered in early summer with light rosy purple flowers. Use young plants with pliable stems that are easier to train.

An arbour formed of curving ribs joined at the apex can be made to disappear into a wave of planting. Roses are especially beautiful displayed in this way, and one rose trained up each rib very soon makes the planting look self-supporting. A broad arch will be needed to support a strong-growing rose, and the proportions should be sufficiently generous that thorns are not a problem. You will also need to leave adequate room for access around the rear for maintenance – the classic rose arbour is a substantial garden feature, not an inconspicuous nest, and it should be positioned and planned for accordingly.

That done, there is the joy of choosing the roses themselves. Just a few suggestions (all scented) would be: *R.* 'Albertine', with double flowers in varied pink-peach tones; *R.* 'Wedding Day', which has single blooms in clusters, white with a lemony tinge; *R.* 'Alister Stella Gray', bearing sprays of buttery coloured flowers with a rich tea scent; the pearly *R.* 'Awakening' (syn. *R.* 'Probuzini'), a sumptuous, fully double sport of *R.* 'New Dawn'; and *R.* 'Sophie's Perpetual', which is a shorter variety with double flowers in deep pink fading to pale pink in the middle. Double white flowers festoon *R.* 'Swan Lake', while the blooms on *R.* 'Climbing Sombreuil' are creamier in tone. I especially like the peachy tones of *R.* 'Meg' intermingled with burgundy and rich purple flowers.

Some roses will happily flower all summer and on into the autumn without much attention – the salmon pink *R.* 'Phyllis Bide' and *R.* 'Paul's Perpetual White' oblige in this way – but others will need help along the way with regular dead-heading.

To prolong the seasonal and, therefore, visual interest of arches and arbours mix in some evergreen support material and climbers that provide colour in other seasons. An evergreen honeysuckle, such as *Lonicera japonica* 'Halliana', will provide some clothing to a framework all year as well as summer scent after early roses. Alternatively, in a sheltered position the large, glossy foliage of *Clematis armandii* will give a year-round cloak of green and large clusters of scented white flowers in the spring; it will need to be tied into a sturdy structure. The Chilean potato tree (*Solanum crispum* 'Glasnevin') continues reliably on through the summer and looks fine partnered with any dark-foliaged climber. For a late summer combination, I like to use a deciduous honeysuckle, either *Lonicera tragophylla* or *L. etrusca*

'Superba', to host *Clematis × durandii*, a lax, semi-herbaceous clematis with stormy blue flowers that remind me of bottles of school ink. *Clematis × triternata* 'Rubromarginata' is a lively performer in late summer, bearing interesting, dizzy little cruciform flowers of white margined with maroon, but its real selling point is the fragrance that remains hanging in the air.

An arbour clothed with climbers that can be seen from indoors should looks good in winter, too. Give a seasonal lift with a container planted with a clipped evergreen and a succession of bulbs. On the other hand, it might be refreshing to see the stark change of its skeleton emerge after the leaves fall in autumn. A wigwam of hazel rods enclosing a comfortable seat, which has been a support for sweet peas and runner beans all summer, is no less a visual attraction when it is stripped to its bones through the winter.

Coping with climbing roses

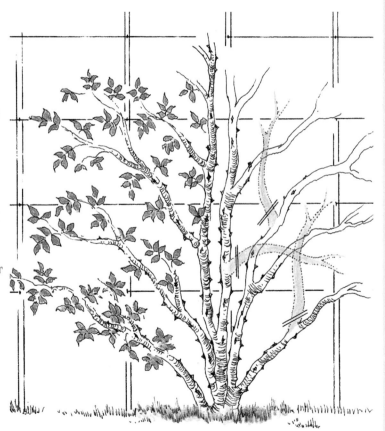

Climbing roses on arches require good management and attention to prevent them from getting out of hand and dangerously top-heavy. Make sure that the arbour is sheltered from the wind, as weight of planting can bring down the whole lot in stormy weather. Avoid roses with huge growth that can have a stiff habit and are unwieldy and awkward to deal with – *Rosa filipes* 'Kiftsgate' would be a disaster, but *R.* 'Paul's Himalayan Musk' gives a similar effect with a slightly pinker tone and is more manageable. *R.* 'Aimée Vibert', which has sprays of scented double white blooms, would be a candidate for smaller arches. Pillar roses, such as the vibrant crimson *R.* 'Dublin Bay' and the pretty pink *R.* 'Aloha', have a flexible habit and growth rate that restricts their ultimate height to between 2 and 3m (6–10ft).

It is important that all main shoots are twisted around their support as low as possible to promote full growth around the base before training the growth upwards. Supports will look uncomfortably naked around the base if this first step is ignored. Tie in the shoots with twine or rose ties making sure that the growth does not cross. Do not use wire or nylon string, which will cut into the stems, causing breakages. Start to prune when the plant has reached the height required. Cut back the side shoots that flowered during the previous year as well as some of the unproductive main growth, together, of course, with all dead and diseased material.

▷▷ Branches of young trees can be laced together to form a living, woven arbour that glistens and trembles in the breeze. Choose the small-leaved lime (*Tilia cordata*) or a decorative whitebeam, such as *Sorbus aria* 'Lutescens', to enjoy foliage with a silver-grey underside.

Living arches

Just as a hedge may be thought of as a 'living fence', so hedging plants can make very successful 'living arbours'. Beech and hornbeam, that are so nearly evergreen but also have a seasonal highlight, are both attractive and trouble free. Keep clipping to extend the juvenile state and there will be hardly any bare branches. Use it as a semi-enclosed seat in a town garden, where it will be an absorbing clipped shell with the sound of rustling leaves helping to mask outside noise.

Living arches make fine bowers on their own or they can be 'decorated' with light climbers. Yew (*Taxus baccata*) is classically used as a dark green support for the scarlet-flowered flame creeper (*Tropaeolum speciosum*). This perennial climber, which enjoys a dampish environment and prefers its roots in shade and in a well-prepared, humus-rich soil, probably will not reach much past eye level but it will travel gracefully up the sides. In contrast, sweet peas will race upwards, as long as there is a good system of supports. The perennial everlasting pea (*Lathyrus latifolius*) will easily reach 2m (6ft) in height, making it a good candidate for quick and easy screening for a new arch. Soft pink and white forms have an ethereal appearance at dusk − *L. l.* 'White Pearl' has larger flowers and is a show-stopper. Sweet peas are easy enough to raise from seed, and they will cover the side of a garden building that is well blanketed in chicken wire without assistance, but you might need to guide the tendrils to attach themselves to a green, living arch. In dry spells they will probably also need some shade and moisture for the roots in this situation.

Trailing annual nasturtiums (*Tropaeolum majus*) have a rambling growth pattern and are less brittle; those varieties with strong yellow and orange tones look quite exotic matched with vivid red or deep blue flowering climbers and wall shrubs. Their habit of rambling at will makes them ideal partners for other climbing plants grown from seed, such as the vigorous cup-and-saucer vine (*Cobaea scandens*), which has dramatic, deep purple bells. Let them grow wherever they like − after all, management doesn't matter because they'll all be pulled out at the end of the season. Morning glory (*Ipomoea tricolor* 'Heavenly Blue') can mingle with vibrant oranges and pinks, or it looks well twining up among toning blue foliage − threading skywards through *Cupressus arizonica* var. *glabra*, for example, or silver leaves (*Vitis vinifera* 'Incana' springs to mind again). The dark burgundy bellflowers of *Rhodochiton atrosanguineus* give a shadowy look around the sides of an arch, while the soft scarlet of the Chilean glory vine (*Eccremocarpus scaber* f. *carmineus*) needs a dense base plant that will absorb the rather untidy, frilly foliage. Providing full colour and good upward growth, runner beans create their own seasonal living arch, light-hearted and fruitful.

Private eyries

Fun is often forgotten in outdoor planning. We can get horribly sentimental about our gardens, so the odd quirky structure can be a relief. Of course, to overplay that would negate the small joke. In Tudor times trees were used as private roosting places, housing platforms and ladders, and the smallest private hiding places can still

be among living forms, topiary canopies of yew or under the more natural skirts of a weeping willow – a special childhood memory.

Constructing a private hideaway above eye level has an added bonus of being a double-tiered, useful space as well as a secluded retreat. An old specimen tree would make a marvellous roost, its existing overhead canopy already forming a screen overhead. Nowadays, few gardens have a suitable tree to house a look-out or eyrie, but you can develop this idea of taking yourself up and away from being on show by building a free-standing structure that appears to be fixed to a tree or

A WILLOW ARBOUR

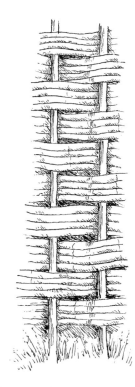

△ Willow (*Salix* spp.) can be used to make a living arbour. Use it for the staves and interweave pliable shoots to form the sides.

THE advantage of a living arbour is primarily that nature is close at hand. The foliage will rustle around you and create effects with light and shade, providing a comforting, sheltered environment. Willow has always been useful to all forms of animal life. It used to be considered 'sacred' to humans and is valuable in ecological terms for wildlife. It provides shelter as it grows and is a natural material for screening in simple panel form, as hurdles, as well as for buildings. This renewable resource not only grows fast but it will strike fast from green shoots, or withies, of *Salix triandra* or *S. purpurea*, plunged into the ground. The pliable green shoots can be interwoven around larger stakes of *S. viminalis*, which, although it makes the fastest growth, is not flexible enough for weaving. Because willow enjoys a moist soil, these stakes have the advantage of not rotting in the ground. In no time at all, you can be sitting in a living basket that blends completely into the background.

looks part of the overall effect. With its gnarled, twisted form, a free-standing wisteria is a good subject for this treatment.

One branch alone cannot support a tree house, but hardwood posts concreted into the ground and braced can form the foundation and framework of your 'nest'. Even a structure that is only 1m (3ft) off the ground can feel sufficiently screened, as long as there is extra bulk from a substantial tree trunk or canopy to provide a partial cloak. You will be able to increase privacy with low sides encasing the frame plus a pitched roof to keep off rain. If young children are on the scene, a balustrade of railings or poles for safety will be essential. Watch out for the condition of the tree, because, as with all living things, it needs to keep growing – the branches will fill out and foliage can change its character.

To integrate your eyrie into its supporting tree, plant some climbers to scramble upwards or, if there is sufficient room for their roots to spread, add young trees around the structure.

Planted nests

All this talk about construction and hard elements might have thrown out the challenge for you to create a little world that is entirely plant-led as well as being more economical. You will also have gathered together some ideas about what really suits you and your garden. Using plants alone to create a private space gives you the opportunity to let your imagination take over and conjure up brushstrokes of images, sounds and scent remembered. I believe that gardens are an art form in which, although function certainly plays an important role, some part of the plot should be an area where you can dream without disturbance amid living things. Unlike the practical divisions in Chapter 4, the pattern or geometry of these intimate places is relatively unimportant, so informal curves might develop, edges will be undefined, swathes of planting will emerge like a whisper and any overheads are living things, even if they are supported invisibly.

I work in a garden where the owner has spent her lifetime helping children, and, although she has no children of her own, young relatives visit often. Over time, small areas of this garden have developed into centres of childhood play. Within a small wood a slight depression in the earth, caused by felling a tree, was scooped out to make a shallow saucer. It is carpeted with ivy (the shoots pegged down initially to encourage new roots to take) and the remaining stump, on the perimeter, provides a focus for a swirl of the soft shield fern (*Polystichum setiferum*). It sounds too simple, but the idea is that nothing fancy should get in the way of running down into this saucer and collapsing in a heap on a soft spread of leaves – green in spring and summer, with a top

△ This shady retreat among the treetops is just large enough for one. A sturdy support system is crucial.

▷ A leafy green oasis can be tucked away in even small gardens. Structural planting of bamboo, fatsia, choisya and viburnum ensures a degree of privacy at all times.

dressing of crackly brown in autumn and winter – or just lying there, quite hidden, staring up at the canopy overhead. As the canopy is mature beech, nothing much succeeds below it, but in late spring a mass of bluebells shimmer around the rim of this simple bowl.

On the edge of this same little piece of woodland, the light reaches in and touches the ground, so we made an 'armchair' space, semi-enclosed with a horseshoe of native hedging, and placed an old log to face towards the bright fields – somewhere to play or simply to sit and gaze outwards. The floor is carpeted with a mix of lavender-blue wood anemone (*Anemone nemorosa* 'Robinsoniana'), scented white violets (*Viola cornuta* Alba Group) and the dark, nodding flowers of *Geranium phaeum*.

At the core of this small wood is the largest beech tree, where long ropes support an elegant swing suspended over sweeps of low bulbs, including winter aconite (*Eranthis hyemalis*) and *Crocus tommasinianus*, which erupt from the grass in a succession of coloured swirls before early summer brings the fresh green foliage overhead that doesn't need any competition from colour on the ground. Sitting on this swing, you're oblivious to anything but the motion of swing against the overhead branches as you look up, or the carpet beneath as you gaze down – a tiny private paradise that grew out of nothing more than the fortuitous position of a sturdy beech bough.

This example shows, above all else, how ideas for secluded, private areas develop out of an image, and how established planting can help to trigger ideas. Trees provide a useful starting point – not only do they screen from above, but they provide a base or focus around which to create. You could use them as a support for roses to cascade overhead, and this is, for once, the setting for the white clouds of the mammoth *R. filipes* 'Kiftsgate', or for *R.* 'Bobbie James' or *R.* 'Rambling Rector', which are especially splendid spraying out of tall conifers. Where you have limited space, be circumspect about your choice (suggestions for climbers in smaller gardens are given in the Plant Directory).

An established tree is not a prerequisite, however. You might be fortunate enough to be able to make use of an overhanging branch from an neighbouring garden – do ask before you do this – or you could even buy a specimen tree to give an instant effect, although this will need heavy staking and appear rather obviously new for a good long while.

More effective, and eventually more satisfactory, is to plant a very small grove or group of young trees – just three will give the required effect and look more informal than a pair. Plant them close, so that the canopies intermingle; or position one slightly apart from its neighbours to provide a focus when you are relaxing below. Trees with light growth, such as silver birch (*Betula pendula*), are almost more beautiful before the leaves fill out and look well underplanted with clumps of dark burgundy-flowered hellebores and spreads of snowdrops. A small-growing grey alder (*Alnus incana* 'Laciniata'), with delicate cut foliage, would make a base for a waterside retreat. The upright hawthorns (*Crataegus* spp.) and varieties of rowan (*Sorbus* spp.) are ideal choices for their fast growth and attractive foliage – and, of course, their showy fruits. *Sorbus aucuparia* 'Fructu Luteo', with yellow autumn berries, or the more slender *S. hupehensis* and *S. vilmorinii* are perfect for close planting. Keep the underplanting simple, especially if you wish to lie on the ground without crushing any treasures:

A tough customer

Periwinkle (*Vinca* spp.) is one of the few flowering ground-cover plants tough and dependable enough to spring back after being trampled. The variegated form, *V. major* 'Variegata', will smother most weeds and spread vigorously. More delicate and attractive are the variegated forms of *V. minor* – 'Argenteovariegata' and 'Alba Variegata' – which look refreshing but need encouragement to develop into a good spread. The shiny green leaves remain with us all year, and it is quite happy in shade, although sun will be needed to encourage the flowers – which may vary from the original sky blue from white through mauve to plum, and can be single or double.

◁ Nestling alone among plants can be idyllic when the surroundings are a light woodland glade like this, with slim shafts of birch (*Betula* spp.) fringed with blue poppies (*Meconopsis* × *sheldonii*), the round pompons of the guelder rose (*Viburnum opulus*) and spires of white foxgloves (*Digitalis purpurea* f. *albiflora*).

MINIATURE WOODLAND RETREATS

T HESE are two examples of how a secluded glade could be created around one base tree. More than anything, the aim is to build up an atmospheric little world that you enter, not a pretty composition to be viewed from face on. The base trees have been chosen to suit contrasting conditions, and the suggestions for the surrounding planting are very mix and match, depending on the type of escape you want to create.

In a small garden a single specimen would be enough, accompanied by just a few of the suggested support plants. With space for three or more of the base tree you might, quite naturally, want to go to town on the planting combinations, but start slowly and add or take away selectively. Both a dense mixture or restrained repetition of a few varieties would work but each would result in quite different effects – which is how it should be.

Light shade

In a shady setting with a humus-rich soil ranging from neutral to acid, a suitable base tree would be *Eucryphia* × *nymansensis* 'Nymansay'. This fairly upright evergreen tree gives a spectacular late-summer display of clear white, cupped flowers, which show up beautifully against foliage with a glossy surface and a grey reveal. To please the senses a basic colour theme of green, white and blue has been chosen, with the odd touch of pink, red and even yellow to jolt. The transitory waves of scent

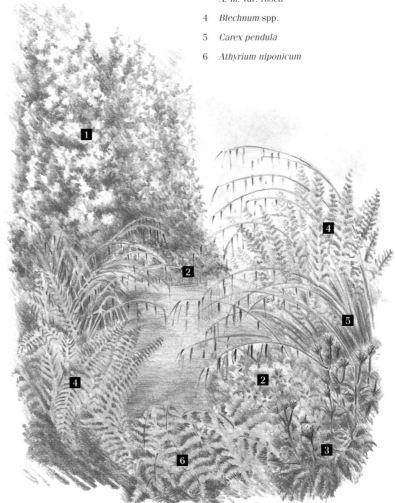

1　*Eucryphia* × *nymansensis* 'Nymansay'

2　*Campanula latifolia*

3　*Astrantia major* var. *rubra* or *A. m.* var. *rosea*

4　*Blechnum* spp.

5　*Carex pendula*

6　*Athyrium niponicum*

△ Planting for a light shade

combined with added visual interest, mainly springing up though the ground-cover carpet, create a cool oasis that is not too exotic.

Support planting includes snowdrops (*Galanthus nivalis*) in late winter, followed by *Anemone blanda* 'Atrocaerulea' and *Erythronium* 'White Beauty' (which is just as its name suggests), with *Helleborus orientalis* in white and pinky green shades for a little extra height. White Siberian squill (*Scilla sibirica* 'Alba') and the Lent lily (*Narcissus pseudonarcissus*) appear through drifts of the rough green leaves of *Pulmonaria angustifolia* subsp. *azurea*, with its vivid blue flowers, or the darker *P. a.* 'Munstead Blue'; *P. longifolia* has less brilliant flower colour but more interesting silver-spotted foliage.

For a little more height, to link ground to tree canopy and also to bring perfume up around your shoulders, add *Lonicera tatarica*, a shrubby honeysuckle or, its lilac-scented relation, *L. rupicola* var. *syringantha*, which flowers a little earlier.

Lily-of-the-valley (*Convallaria majalis*) will fill the air with its scent, and *Tulipa sprengeri* will add graceful flashes of red petals through the longer grass.

Trilliums spread over the ground and ferns unfurling up through them will create small divisions, their fronds forming a backcloth to blue Himalayan poppies (*Meconopsis* × *sheldonii*). Sedge (*Carex pendula*) will add movement through the grove and, at its edge is *Gillenia trifoliata*, planted where the light will display the lacy, arching quality of this delightful treasure.

At the end of summer, delicate spires of campanula, astrantia and aconitum (all of which tolerate light shade) will draw your gaze upwards, towards the flowering of the eucryphia. After this, there is only the gentle quiet of winter shadows falling across the grass.

An open, sunnier situation

In a more open situation a suitable base tree would be *Amelanchier lamarckii*. One of my favourites, it is amenable to most soils as long as there is sufficient depth of topsoil. It can tolerate some shade and is decorative in every season – even in winter the rangy metallic grey stems (it can be grown as a single-stemmed tree but is more usually multi-stemmed) have a sculptural quality.

For the senses colours drift from the fresh white of spring into soft blue-mauves in summer before exploding into terracotta, orange and red to match the amelanchier's leaves. Contrasting colour appears in intermittent flashes.

There is perfume from flowers but also aromatic foliage, and soft, fluffy grassheads to stroke.

Given retentive soil, the support planting is a carpet of snake's head fritillaries (*Fritillaria meleagris*) to accompany the amelanchier's racemes of starry white flowers. To echo the tones of the tree's emerging leaves – papery ovals that flutter in any breeze – are deep purple and wine red bobbles of *Allium atropurpureum* and *A. sphaerocephalon*. Blue spires of camassia provide vertical interest, and ox-eye daisy (*Leucanthemum vulgare*) runs through long grass. Include sweet rocket (*Hesperis matronalis*) to bring a ghostly, almost luminous effect and sweet perfume from dusk through the evening.

In drier situations aromatic woody shrubs – phlomis, sage and, of course, lavender – define the space and are an underplanting for large scented shrub roses: *Rosa moyesii*, which bears small but strongly coloured pink flowers, *R.* 'Nevada', which will have a second flush of creamy flowers, and the good yellow *R.* 'Frühlingsgold'. More tall plants create a loose barrier: the statuesque plume poppy, *Macleaya microcarpa* 'Coral Plume' (a friendly thug in clay soil) and ornamental grasses – miscanthus is as dominating as the plume poppy but plays with any movement of air more effectively.

Perennials to continue the theme through the summer include *Geranium pratense* 'Mrs Kendall Clarke', *Phlox* 'Prospero' or *P.* 'Franz Schubert', which bring blue flashes through clump-forming grasses such as *Calamagrostis* spp. and *Panicum virgatum* 'Rubrum' (watch this come alight in autumn). Add lilies for scent. The herbaceous *Clematis heracleifolia* var. *davidiana* will wend its way vigorously over earlier flowering shrubs and create another level of screening as well as bringing more blue tones and a lavender scent.

For later in the season, add some decorative grassheads: fluffy brushes of *Stipa tenuissima* or, in damper soil, the softly waving threads of *Deschampsia cespitosa* 'Bronzeschleier' (which tolerates light shade) to accompany the coppery tones of *Achillea* 'Terracotta' and *A.* 'Forncett Fletton', which, with *Rosa moyesii*'s red flagon hips and the flushed *Panicum* spp., will herald full autumn, when the amelanchier turns to an orange-red glow and burns itself out, ready to regenerate in spring.

a carpet of periwinkle (*Vinca* spp.) or nothing but grass enlivened in spring by small early bulbs.

Fruiting trees bring to mind orchards – seeking privacy up among the branches or lolling in long grass below – but beware of choosing a juicy-fruited tree. The mulberry tree (*Morus* spp.) is the worst culprit for dropping large, soft fruit over a wide area, and the juice stains badly. In a heavy-cropping year crab apples (*Malus*) could also be a problem.

Just to mention hazel or nut copses often causes gasps of anticipated delight – just one, two or three bushes of *Corylus avellana* will provide a definite atmosphere, with lamb's tail catkins in spring and cobnuts in autumn. Underplant with primroses and bluebells interspersed with ferns in pools of shade – in a damp area try the lady's fern (*Athyrium filix-femina*), which sprays out tall fronds in spring.

I like to feel and hear the wind in the trees, so my light canopy would be aspen (*Populus tremula*), with foliage that flutters to show the white underside. These fast-growing, slim trees respond well to pollarding, which could be necessary in a smaller garden.

Tall shrubs that are relatively fast-growing can quickly make a secluded glade in an open situation. Philadelphus or a shrubby honeysuckle such as *Lonicera fragrantissima* will provide scent and a lower screen against which to sit. The buddleias *Buddleja crispa* and *B. fallowiana* bear scented racemes, while *B. davidii* is tougher and stronger growing but equally spectacular, although in a coarser form. The butterflies that are attracted to buddleias are a worthwhile bonus, and could be given further encouragement from an underplanting of another butterfly attractor, *Sedum spectabile*.

In a wild garden, old man's beard (*Clematis vitalba*) and woodbine or the wild honeysuckle (*Lonicera periclymenum*) could be left to weave through each other, mounding up into a soft, downy hedge; add decorative height and contrast without straying too far from the untamed with *Anthriscus sylvestris* 'Ravenswing', a striking dark purple form of cow parsley.

Colours will be important in these intimate areas. You could pick up on the flower or berry colour of a tree and follow through; the orange berries of rowan, for example, echoed in some brilliant day lilies, *Hemerocallis fulva* 'Flore Plena', or the mauve-pink berries of *Sorbus vilmorinii* picked up in a barrier screen of bear's breeches (*Acanthus mollis*). Purple-headed alliums to anticipate these late summer colours would contribute a contrast in form with their seedheads.

Complementary textures can occur in the ground-cover pattern, with the delicate heart-shaped foliage of epimedium and the rounded leaf of ajuga – both evergreens that appreciate dappled shade. Clumps of the greater woodrush (*Luzula sylvatica*) will just catch the breeze, and the variegated form makes a brilliant small highlight, especially against a solid background. Spring bulbs, such as scented narcissi, would provide another reason for lingering.

The most natural little retreat you can devise is barely planted at all – a mown circle in a swathe of long grass – but it fulfils the requirements with which we began the chapter: it is somewhere peaceful and intimate, where you can relax and be undisturbed. How you get there is up to you – you might be inclined to devise a drawbridge.

6 | DISTRACTING THE EYE

DRAWING the attention away from eyesores beyond the boundaries to a pleasing image inside the garden is a successful solution to a difficult problem. This distraction can be achieved by keeping all emphasis and interest at ground level, at night by subtle lighting or even, as on a stage set, by illusion. But the most adaptable 'trick' is to use a strong focal point to grab the attention. This might be a bold plant, a planter or series of containers drawing your attention towards a particular view or a striking piece of sculpture. These can all hold the attention if well chosen and well sited, but for real absorbing interest, nothing can compete with water and lighting. Although they require time and money to install, these are the most satisfying and compelling features to distract the eye.

Using focal points

Any feature intended to attract attention should be selectively chosen and placed with discretion. To overdo focal points and features makes the eye restless and so defeats the objective. 'Very selective, more effective' is a useful maxim. Wrongly placed, such features can obstruct the use of a space and can seem so obvious that the space is not explored and people walk straight past. Instead, they should just encourage movement into the space.

With easily movable objects, it is advisable to try out placements and even mock up possibilities and live with them for a

◁◁ Symmetrical spheres of neatly clipped box (*Buxus* spp.) reinforce the role of the statue and encourage the eye towards it. In late summer the chalky white flowers of *Anemone × hybrida* 'Honorine Jobert' provide glimmering highlights.

△ The contrasting foliage details of the iris and lady's mantle (*Alchemilla mollis*) are intrinsic to this little composition.

▷ Strong, well-executed patterns on the ground are certain to capture and hold the attention. The swirl of fragmented dark slate supports a rim of intricate planting textures.

while just to make sure the effect works. Objects that appear substantial inside shops and showrooms often look lost outside, where natural light, the expanse of sky, extraneous sound and the movement of plants and clouds can minimize and seemingly reduce their stature. In the same vein, it is a mistake to use features suitable for a larger garden by reducing their scale to fit a smaller site. Never be afraid of maintaining great simplicity and style in small spaces.

Using temporary or movable focal points is an invaluable way of providing a short-term distraction while waiting for other screening to grow and provide more permanent concealment and shelter. Containers, recycled or inexpensive ornaments and quick-growing plants are all items that can be moved and be rehoused elsewhere when privacy is complete without being too much of a shock on the pocket.

Ornament for attention

Some say that a garden is incomplete without a piece of sculpture; others suggest that a garden should not contain an object that is not alive. Each to his own, but a grand statue on a plinth is suited only to a limited number of situations – a row of stone balls placed at the base of a wall, their horizontal line keeping interest inside the garden, might be an easier sculptural statement to live with. Pieces of hewn stone or boulders tooled to form seats make large ornamental features, while collections of pebbles, watering cans or even glass bottles are more intimate ornaments that will nevertheless fascinate. A simple piece of driftwood from the beach that is left lounging across the terrace will firmly direct the eye across in a sweep. Improvised, recycled paraphernalia can provide an opportunity for humour as long as it is a point of interest and the scale is correct – too large or too small will make a disquieting feature.

In a small garden an ornament is best sited near or in the planting to avoid cluttering up valuable space and to make as much of the feature as possible. Partially screening it from some angles also means that its role is exploited to the full. In a larger urban garden you might choose to associate an ornament with a pergola or with trellis panels in a traditional fashion or incorporate it into an illusory background for a more strongly three-dimensional effect. In a country garden, choose a form that sits well in the surroundings – animal sculptures of woven wire and willow reflect rural life.

Furniture as a focal point

Garden furniture can also double as ornament, its invitation to relax underlining what privacy in the garden is all about.

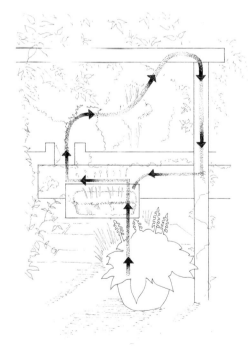

△ The careful placing of focal points can direct the eye around a site until it eventually comes to rest on a chosen point.

▷ 'Found' driftwood with exaggerated decoration becomes a
functional as well as an aesthetic
garden object.

Unfortunately, seating chosen for its eye-catching shape is often quite uncomfortable – moulded fibreglass can feel very hot and sticky, while stone benches are cold
and cast iron benches are hard to sit on, even with cushions. However, as long as
they are not intended to be the only thing you can sit on, they provide attractive
focal points. I have a garden bench that is almost completely smothered with *Rosa*
'Nevada' – there have been complaints, but I'm afraid I like it like that.

Circular seats ringing a tree trunk can turn any tree into a scene-stealer. They
smack of the grand life and are difficult places to hold a conversation, but a large
garden requires suitably large features. You could set one around a specimen tree
to catch the eye or use it in a secluded spot from which you have shelter and shade
at any time of the day – just move yourself around the circle to avoid the sun.

Seating of all types needs a background wall, fence or planting as, quite hon-
estly, it feels cosier to sit with your back against some bulk rather than to be stuck
out in the open.

Containers

Whether they are planted up or not, containers can be very effective focal points.
A thoughtfully placed container draws the eye into a well-screened corner or background, using an upright shape for impact, or keeping the eye down with a lower,
chunkier form. A pair of matching containers, symmetrically positioned, will mark
an entrance to a garden within a garden; a series around a covered eating area will

help 'root' it into the surrounding planting and give extra structure and solidity. Remember they need to do this job satisfactorily from inside as well as outside. In a long, narrow plot, containers placed in offset positions, either side of the main axis, provide a focus on the journey down the garden.

In a restricted area, where repetition of a strong shape is an important element of the design, choose a focal container to reflect other elements in the garden – smooth and rounded to echo the shape of a circular pool or grassed area; slatted wood to tie in well with fencing; angular to underline the effect of squares or rectangles in the ground pattern. Four matching square containers, either placed one in each corner of a square paved area or grouped together on it, centrally or just off-centre, will strengthen the overall design to a surprising degree.

Giving a container or group of containers a contrasting 'mat' on which to stand will give added impact. Consider inset paving slabs in a gravel surface, a pattern of pebbles in a brick surface or introducing some evergreen ground-cover to nestle around the base – ivy, periwinkle, ferns or violas for a shady position; thymes, low sedum or alpine phlox in the sun.

Inexpensive, lightweight containers can be painted or covered with fragments of china, glass and mirrors to become eye-catching features in their own right. A light-hearted treatment of these containers enables you to have fun positioning them. Spread them out in a wave or stagger them to make a pattern. Make a game out of the placing. This form of image will provide a focus all year. Planting in such bright containers will need to be kept simple – something plain but strong such as pittosporum or × *Fatshedera lizei* will give a positive effect.

Where a container is used alone as a sculptural feature, the shape and form, material and colour must all contribute; they should call attention to themselves and yet be in harmony with the style of the surroundings. A contemporary town garden will require a container that looks at home with the clean lines of hard landscaping – your choice could range from an elegant, black, glazed pot with an organic form to straight-sided, galvanized florist buckets, the hard, shiny finish fitting an up-to-date image and perhaps echoing a metal screen or plant framework. A hand-thrown terracotta pot looks at home in a Mediterranean-style garden or gravel-covered courtyard surroundings, while traditional lead urns fit into a more formal scheme. This underlines the point that, as a form alone, the container needs to complement the neighbouring elements.

The combination of a striking pot and dramatic plant will double the effect. Spiky plants, such as phormiums, cordylines and yuccas, are best set in containers that widen out from a narrow base, reflecting the shape of the plant. These subjects grow well in pots and are sure to attract attention, but they can grow vigorously in enclosed settings, thrusting their foliage, and your gaze, skywards. Add soft, waving, ornamental grasses that soften the image and encourage the eye to follow the slender arching habit downwards again. Position them where the backcloth gives a suitable, unfussy screen, or as part of an internal division, where they will have the space to develop their full dramatic shape.

I use bamboos in movable containers to provide an adjustable screen and a feature at the same time. The foliage moving in the breeze attracts attention and focuses the mind. In this situation, the material for the containers needs to

△ Brimming with personality, a striking container is filled with little treasures, including a fleshy aeonium and red primulas. The delicate blue flowers of *Corydalis flexuosa* 'Père David' tone in well.

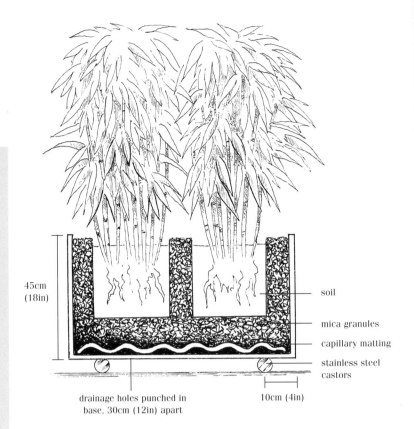

▷ A cross-section of a triangular galvanized zinc container

45cm (18in)

soil

mica granules

capillary matting

stainless steel castors

drainage holes punched in base, 30cm (12in) apart

10cm (4in)

Container care

Uncared-for tubs, with plants flopping over the sides, attract attention for all the wrong reasons. Make sure the base has good drainage, and choose the most suitable compost for the plants you are growing. Use a soil-based mix for pots that have a permanent position, and especially for trees and large shrubs. For pots that are going to be moved around, a peat- or coir-based compost will be much lighter – so light, in fact, that in windy conditions containers may get blown over. Soak the compost thoroughly before planting up, and change the mix more frequently than you would a soil-based compost.

All compost in containers will dry out much more quickly than in the open garden, especially in exposed sites such as roof gardens and balconies. Add a top layer of stone chippings as a mulch to deflect heat and retain moisture; the chippings also provide a smart contrast to foliage.

Vigorous plants that are to spend their lives in pots – the bamboos mentioned above, for example – can be root-pruned, perhaps every other year, to keep them healthy but within bounds. Remove any roots that are visible on the outside of the pot and reduce the thicker roots in the rootball by one-third, teasing out any fibrous roots and removing any loose dead matter. A labour-saving method is to keep such plants in pots within a larger decorative container, with a generous infill of mica granules over capillary matting to cosset them.

complement the texture of the plant, as well as being sufficiently lightweight. Galvanized metal, in curved or angular shapes, fulfils the brief. Small castors fitted underneath will help to make the planted containers mobile.

Pots or tubs of specimen plants that are clipped to shape make forceful statements in formal settings close to buildings. They can be used alone or in a group, with various geometric shapes working together to form a strongly architectural focus.

Plants for centre stage

Plants do not have to be in containers to attract attention, of course. If plants are your passion and you enjoy organizing a succession of plants to deliver impact, then you will surely choose some eye-catching specimens as a focus.

It is important that the characteristics of the plant are used to full advantage. An upright form, for example, should not stand out like a sore thumb; instead, it should be used as a punctuation mark in front of massed foliage. Arching shapes need a home where a breeze can exploit their graceful habit rather than being planted in an exposed spot where the wind will ravage them. Horizontal shapes tend to force the eye away from the plant unless this is cleverly sited – the variegated form of the wedding cake tree (*Cornus controversa* 'Variegata') needs the surrounding bulk of tall shrubs and trees against which to show itself off, when its hovering layers are breathtaking. Gnarled wisteria, the spiralling stems of corkscrew hazel (*Corylus avellana* 'Contorta') or topiary shapes all have a sculptural quality and make quirky talking points, but they are also living things that, unlike static sculptures, are never quite the same year after year.

Strong effects in small spaces

In a limited area the boundary will always form a backcloth for the star of the show, and this can be exploited to good effect. Picture the silvery foliage of mullein (*Verbascum thapsus*) against a dark, timber boundary in a sunny corner, or the cardoon (*Cynara cardunculus*) for a similar effect but twice the size. To impress in a shady position against a light coloured, rendered wall, *Fatsia japonica* would give maximum contrast with its strong, glossy foliage. To lift dark courtyard spaces, the variegated form of the fatsia (*F. j.* 'Variegata') will be useful. However, I prefer a similar, but more interesting specimen, tree ivy (× *Fatshedera lizei* 'Variegata'), to bring punch into low-key areas. Both plants are tolerant of pollution and can be treated as wall shrubs in cramped conditions.

For a classy or fun image, clipped material will also be happy in semi-shade. Topiary shapes are there all year and are great for providing a frame for a delicate spray of Christmas lights. The shapes can be abstract forms of evergreen bulk or aeroplanes, even dolphins, tied into a wire framework to suit any size of garden. Topiary doesn't have to look formal – a garden in Holland has a family of topiarized chickens growing out of a lawn.

Some plants have a natural architectural quality without needing to be shaped. *Acanthus spinosus* erupts from the ground with great aplomb and would be equally effective as a punctuation point in a border or rising in stately isolation out of gravel. The honey bush (*Melianthus major*) needs a sheltered site, but in the right position it rewards with large glaucous leaves that advance upwards in layers to over 2m (6ft) – the plant is an interesting paradox of stateliness and absolute informality. All the spiky forms that suit container growing – phormiums, cordylines and yuccas – will made strong statements, and the variegated forms in particular will leap forward visually to demand attention. Given a hot sunny position, in open ground they will attain substantial height and spread – say 2 to 3m (6–10ft). The spikes will form into arching fans that look absolutely stunning in a gentle breeze with companion planting of smaller, round-leaved species, such as pittosporum, corokia and sedum.

The ideas for green walls suggested in Chapter 2 can be extended to making a eye-catching feature instead of a backdrop. A red-flushed vine tied into red trellis would make a truly arresting picture, while the rampaging golden-leaved hop (*Humulus lupulus* 'Aureus') grows up from nothing each year to form a cascade of golden or lime green foliage. The large hand-shaped leaves of a trained fig fanned out against a warm wall is a splendid sight and wonderfully aromatic. Equally impressive but quite different in character is the soft foliage of *Actinidia kolomikta*, each heart-shaped leaf graduating from green through white to pink, as mouth-watering as strawberries and cream.

Feature plants in larger gardens

Where there is room, you might wish to use small trees to attract attention away from surrounding buildings. Where the complete form of the tree can be seen, it would be preferable to choose one with a spreading or weeping habit so that your line of sight is encouraged along the curve back down into the garden. Evergreens, of course, will give their unchanging solidity throughout the year. Many deciduous varieties can offer eye-catching qualities in different seasons: the brilliant autumn colour of the stag's horn sumach *(Rhus typhina)*, followed by its strong winter 'antlers'; the gleaming trunks of white-stemmed birches and the peeling bark cherry (*Prunus serrula*), which does exactly what it says and sheds its old bark to reveal a glowing mahogany skin that just clamours to be stroked (proud owners have been known to have polished them).

At a lower level – in height but not in interest – ornamental grasses and bamboos take a lot of beating. Many are at their peak visually in winter and, when they are given room to develop, the larger types such as pampas grass (*Cortaderia selloana*) and eulalia (*Miscanthus sinensis*) will reward with fountains 3m (10ft) high and across. Use one plant as a specimen, three or more for a completely stunning effect. Golden oats (*Stipa gigantea*) lives up to its name and its oat-like tassels, waving royally above all its neighbours, will make an uncomplaining and very effective disguise for a dull fence for much of the year.

Winter attractions are to be especially cherished, and if you have an area of damp ground, certain varieties of dogwood (*Cornus* spp.) look dynamic planted in spreads. Winter sunshine will bring a glow to their bare, coloured stems, but even in gloomy weather the upright straps are visually arresting. Primary tones of red, yellow and rather elegant black make diverting coloured swatches at the end of a plot and beside an ornamental pool or natural pond. When interest is low during the darker months, these accommodating plants will keep your attention away from depressing aspects.

When the soil warms up and pool life wakes up, the large-leaved waterside plants will emerge into their glory. Giant rhubarb (*Gunnera manicata*) is a true giant you cannot ignore, with foliage that even adults are able to stand beneath. Slightly smaller than *Gunnera manicata*, but just as impressive is a form of the ornamental rhubarb, *Rheum palmatum* 'Atrosanguineum'. Flushes of deep red stain the underside of the leaves and show again in the flower plumes. Trees to accompany this drama have to have great character. This is the right home for the weeping willow (*Salix* × *sepulcralis* var. *chrysocoma*), which needs to have at least 10m (30ft) all around it and must be planted well away from any building in order to put on its full, magnificent show.

Patterns on the ground

To form noticeable patterns in an expanse of hard landscaping is a tried and tested method of creating interest down at ground level. Both hard landscaping and planting can bring an enclosing mood to a space or encourage the eye to travel in a purposeful direction.

In the worst circumstances, where all the surrounding aspects seem to penetrate your privacy, you will be reliant on stunning and compelling features that

focus the eye down as much as possible. Strong horizontal lines, from tiered planting or strings of low hedging, will help, but real success will come from a firm
ground pattern and perhaps a simple, but strongly shaped water feature to draw the
gaze down and hold it there, to be all absorbing and meditative.

Some ornamental elements can be used in the hard pattern, as a perimeter band
or to enhance the central space – now all those pebbles collected on the beach can
have a permanent home. There should be one predominant material with which
the subordinate textures fit in, like rugs on a floorboard base; keep details and
embellishments low-key and be bold with the overall impact – small-scale elements
work well in large-scale arrangements here.

There are numerous ways in which collections of simple natural elements can
be used to personalize a pedestrian element and serve to direct or attract attention.
A few timber strips used horizontally as detail across a larger expanse of brick laid
end to end will seemingly expand the space; stone aggregate will integrate well
around the staggered edges and infill into planted areas.

Use the inherent character of a material to its best advantage and discover the
variety of effect that can be obtained from a single material. Brick can be laid in
many bonds to make many patterns, either bed faced or on edge, and although
flowing sweeps create a strong sense of movement, it still has a rigidity of form that
can be exploited in pattern making to give a crisp and correct formality for a traditional appearance. Unless you really want a crumbly, very weathered look to
your detailing, choose bricks and paviours that are frost resistant; they will be more
uniform and easier to handle.

Clay tiles, gently mixed in with brick and gravel, will make an informal wave
across a hard landscaped area. Wooden setts cut from treated garden posts are a
good alternative to the harder granite rock. Very small, sliced rounds of timber also
work well.

Incorporate unexpected ornamental materials to interest and contrast: thin ribs
of metal, bedded glass fragments, black ceramic. Pennies fixed in cement sounds
unnatural but they look fine. Terracotta, ammonites, geology stones, silvery
ormers and black knapped flints, laid in twisting lines with quartz, mica, barnacles
and pearl oysters, can form beautifully textured carpets interlaid with paving. Lay
the large slabs first to form the grid and then infill with the smaller units.

Don't dismiss concrete as a possibility. Instead of looking at pre-cast slabs, consider having it cast on site to any shape, colour and surface texture. Quite angular,
modernistic forms that are unavailable in pre-cast shapes can jigsaw together or be
spread apart to lead the eye off in a certain direction. Coloured dyes can be added
to the mix, uniformly or in spots, swirls and clouds, creating a wonderful, patterned
carpet. The surface finish can be scored, brushed or scrubbed before it has completely gone off to expose the aggregate or it can be spread with a sprinkling of
pebbles or coloured stones to give a stronger skin. Scrubbed white, aggregate,
freeform shapes associate well with the cloudy, dark tones of slate or earthy quar-
ries. This effect is particularly suited to a contemporary space where strong direc-
tional pattern is needed to avert the gaze from overbearing surroundings.

Black, white and green marble in geometric shapes edged with tiny patterned
tiles, smooth pebbles or strips of slate will bring life to dull, pre-cast slabs. You need

▽ Subtle touches integrated into
the ground surface will be not only
more compelling but also easier
to live with. The sprinkling of
reflective stones is the perfect
touch – imagine the scene at
twilight.

only a little of this detailing to lift an entire spread of uniform slabs. Try this in small spaces, in tiny town backyards or in enclosed front gardens and watch them spring into life.

Pebbles and cobbles make an indigenous and highly decorative aggregate that glistens when wet but gives good grip on an uneven surface. Pebble paths were built into old Chinese gardens, and their charm still attracts. These river stones, in harmonious natural tones, work well grouped and edged with a contrasting strip, and they can give a delightful sense of movement when laid in curving sweeps.

Easy paving patterns can be made with tiles. Terracotta and glazed surfaces, in square, rectangular, octagonal and other geometric shapes, inspire thoughts of hot, dry countries, where pools and canals are intrinsic to the scheme. They look at home in a courtyard setting.

Mosaic tiles in different shapes and colours are often brilliant and striking when laid in bold patterns that can be intricate, but not overworked and fussy. Translucent, polychrome tiles can be used as scattered inserts to show up the opaque, rougher textures, but beware of overdoing the 'hacienda' look and remember they can be slippery. Even bits of household china, found on site, can be used.

Wooden, marquetry-type mosaic is something I would like to see used more often in informal, relaxed environments, where curves and cuts across the grain make patterns. Geometric, timber stepping stones set in chippings can form a strong visual picture. This can steal the scene when the ground-cover is truly tough and able to withstand being walked on. Tiny ivies and periwinkles can successfully mesh together a hard and soft checkerboard.

Remember to include mats of plants as part of the pattern. Aromatic thymes, creeping pennyroyal and tufts of camomile will soften and reshape the hard lines of a paved area, and herbs are at their best when they are allowed to sprawl and creep as they do in nature.

▷ Combining clipped plant forms with hard materials results in a raised pattern, in which light and shade become part of the overall picture.

The spell of water

As a distraction, water wins all the prizes. It can fill many roles: meditative, soothing, uplifting and fun. All these qualities are useful in enhancing your feeling of seclusion in your own outside room. The overriding asset is the sense of relaxation that water conveys. Water with plants has connotations of a desert oasis, where the harsh, unwelcome outside world is banished. Water can provide a focus in many forms, whether as a still pool, reflecting the sky overhead while drawing your attention downwards, as a wildlife pond, forever changing and full of life and interest, or as a lively, splashing feature that, as well as making compulsive viewing, will distract attention from outside noise.

An open pool needs to be in sunlight for at least half a day to maintain a correct biological cycle for the inmates. Shelter from wind is also necessary, although water should be sited away from overhanging trees, if at all possible, because leaf-drop and excessive shade are disadvantages. You will probably want to be able to sit by your water feature, so extra space will need to be allowed or incorporated into the design of the pool itself. Planting around the pool – for shelter, for extra privacy, for integrating into the rest of the garden or for additional sound – will also take up space. Sunken pools, where the water surface is at or below ground level, will need digging out. The cost and disturbance of excavating and removing excess soil from the site can be prohibitive, especially from gardens where access is awkward, and the extra hours of labour involved could cancel out the obvious advantages.

Even if you cannot meet these criteria or are concerned about safety with young children about, you need not go without water in the garden. Water can be a magical answer to backyards where little sun penetrates. A hidden tank may be the answer, perhaps a simple effect of water simply rippling over stones, or as a delicate spray or wall fountain.

Water as a mirror

The flat surface of water will probably be the most compelling part of the garden pattern – even a handkerchief of water becomes a shimmering sheet that glistens and constantly changes. Painting a shallow pool black can make it appear deeper and also hide the base and planting baskets. To bring more attention to a small square of water, give extra detail to its edge, perhaps with tiles set on edge, granite setts, pebble strips or timber – a striking edging will really concentrate the eye. Rectangular shapes will appear to pull the surrounding space out and be an advantage in a narrow garden, where the restrictions beyond the boundary may have forced you into a corner in your search for your much-needed privacy. A narrow, canal-like feature, positioned across the site, will help it seem more spacious. A right-angled pool forming a corner of a private part of the garden will give added seclusion, separating you even more from the neighbouring plot, and one side of this L shape can form a partial division in your own garden. Where space allows, groups of geometric pools laid as parterres are guaranteed to hold your attention. In static pools, where waterlilies will flourish if there is sufficient sun, movement can come from a separate water spout or from fish beneath the surface.

Circular or oval shapes are perfect for inward-looking situations, and they can be ringed by hard paving or a raised 'perching' wall for even greater focus. Any planting in an outer ring will provide a backing screening and help the pool sit well in its surroundings – a curved line of low hedging will suffice in a small space or to create a division in a larger garden.

The country comes to town

If an informal water feature in a built-up area is to appear natural, it needs to 'look' large and, ideally, be sited apart from busy areas, where noise will disturb wildlife. If it is close to buildings, at least one side should be a straight, hard edge. If you find geometry abhorrent, this comment will be difficult to accept, but the firmness of a line of decking or paving will help to anchor the pool in place and enhance the other, more natural edges. I like to use stone, pebbles and gravels with paving or timber to relax and soften the watery shallows. Flat-topped rocks make a good seat for you to turn your back to the world.

A naturalistic water feature should become a complete world for its inhabitants, sited away from noisy neighbours and in a spot where the sun can reach for a small part of the day. A drop in level would make a happy starting point for a gently sloping boggy edge, where large-foliaged marginals would form a screen. In any case, try to develop a small, private area adjacent to the pool, with greenery providing extra screening as well as shelter for wildlife. Your privacy would then be assured with moving foliage and the sounds of the surrounding wildlife.

When does a pool become a pond? Probably when a natural environment becomes established. A wide variety of plants and animals, if only occasional visitors, are at home in an aquatic environment, and even in the middle of a town dragonflies and birds will visit and frogs will move in, to produce tadpoles for succeeding generations.

Water at play

You might prefer to combine water with a sculptural feature that can be seen from more than one aspect, forming a focus in its own right that can leap into life when necessary. Any attractive boulder or piece of natural stone can be drilled through and connected to the pump tubing to allow water to escape and lap down over the surface. This could be combined with an open pool to combine the idea of water and ornament in one focal point. Alternatively, a water boulder could be prominently placed to form part of the terrace or set against a firm backdrop. A millstone with water fanning over the stone in concentric ripples directs your interest to a lower level and, if it is well positioned and integrated, will suit many situations. A broad edging of pebbles disappearing into soft greenery will link it with the planted surroundings and avoid a 'pimple' look.

If you need nothing more than a highlight of interest that comes into play at the flick of a switch, think about a water jet hidden below the paved surface – surprise and pleasure are combined and precious space is hardly affected. You will need a small, sunken water chamber equipped with a pump and spout. The slabs that will cover this area need to be drilled at intervals and then laid on a metal grill over the chamber. The spout is cut level with the finished surface and will need a

◁ Using water as a distraction, even in small spaces, demands a good design with the appropriate scale to make sure that the feature becomes a positive feature in its own right. The honeysuckle *Lonicera japonica* var. *repens* winds through the trellis.

seal to prevent clogging. Pebbles and gravel as a surface will need to be supported on a grid with a finer mesh. A suitable fitment on the spout will give the desired type of spray or bubble. Surface water will find its way into the tank but you will need to keep it topped up to the required level to prevent the pump burning out. These are child-proof and would be suitable as the main feature in a small back-yard or in a divided space in a larger site in sun or shade.

Using copper tubing screwed on to spouts at ground level has a sculptural feel that fits with contemporary outside spaces, and the verdigris finish that appears with time is especially attractive. These musical pipes can be of varying heights to allow the water to bubble gently down or they can be placed to fan out and fitted with a spray nozzle to create a misty arc. With a larger cistern you could experiment with all sorts of effects – without recreating the Trevi fountain. Check that any upright effect doesn't result in attention being drawn up towards unedifying views and also that the drainage area is sufficient.

▷ Personal collections of objects bring individuality and charm to mundane effects. *Iris sibirica* and *Primula japonica* 'Postford White' add flashes of seasonal colour around a pile of ammonites.

Very, very small pools

The neatest water collecting devices in the garden will be groups of bowls as features in busier areas, or bird baths that are better in quieter niches. Standing water, without pumps and fountains to create movement, will still provide a suitably refreshing element and point of interest. The base of any small container – flowerpot saucers, for example – can be spread with colourful gravel, glittering ceramics and marbles, and water plants in containers will attract wildlife. Simple and effective, whether stone, metal, painted plastic or waterproofed timber barrels, these are movable delights that guarantee that attention is drawn down towards ground level, and they are, of course, perfect for roof gardens, where excavation is not possible.

Water features that do not rely on open water have the advantage of being suitable for shade, and they can often look better in dappled shade under an overhanging tree or beneath an overhead screen. They are tactile pieces that welcome inspection.

A wall fountain or water wall will be a main feature in a small space. In a divided garden it would make an obvious focus in one part while contributing its sound even when it is not in sight. Where you plan to use part of the boundary as backing, a thin second-skin wall will be needed to conceal the pipe-work and support the spout fixings. A solid internal division would also be very suitable – a 1m (3ft) drop will be quite sufficient if the scale of the surroundings is appropriate

Decorative masks and wall plaques make amusing spouts for traditional or quirky effects, or you could hide the spout completely – just a gap in brickwork will do – and so create a real element of surprise when the pump is turned on. The water-storage tank can either be incorporated into an unseen rear of the wall or be sunk underground.

A wall down which water falls in a thin, sparkling sheet is an extremely effective variation, especially if there is a mixture of tone and pattern in the brick or stone. Where the wall is rendered concrete, granite and slate trays, ridge tiles or cup-shaped ceramic ledges can be built into the main fabric to produce a cascade effect. Audio-visual orchestration is also possible. The more you break up the water as it falls, the higher the pitch; copper V forms, set in concrete, will also raise the pitch and resonate the sound. The greater the fall of water, the louder the tone, but the clarity is lessened. You might prefer the water to fall as a clean curtain, using a gully that is forced to overflow in a smooth sheet. These water walls will always be dramatic when they are working, but it is important that they are visually successful all the time, so the material and the form of detailing need careful attention.

None of these features is difficult to construct, especially on a small scale, but remember, even if you intend to build your own feature, you will need a qualified electrician to install correct wiring, circuit breakers and sockets for all pumps.

All an illusion

The eye can be easily deceived. Thrusting fastigiate plants will appear to enlarge a space vertically by taking the eye upwards to enjoy the feature beyond. All horizontal forms, hard or soft – the crossbeams of a pergola, stretched rope or taut support for climbers, even the length of the washing line – will push the boundaries outwards, giving the illusion of expanding the width of the garden. Similarly, plants that spread in tiers can appear to give width and also attractively flatten a space, a strange sensation to behold. Of course, it's only a trick of the eye, but it is, nevertheless, a useful tool if you wish to lead the eye across and away.

Large, irregular paving slabs can make an already large space seem huge, especially if they contrast with lively, interesting planting. Making parallel lines – whether of hedges, paths or edges of borders – converge slightly can appear to lengthen the prospect. Natural effects from light and shade can always be exploited to divide and create separate areas and appear to blot out unwanted intrusions. Think about the differences artificial light can make to a room when different combinations are used and how odd corners can take on a new look and atmosphere. This works just as well in a garden.

Mirrored reflections and *trompe-l'oeil* effects can be a little dis-orientating but nevertheless fun – this is the feature of the future. Playing with illusions and manipulating your own images to give short-term attractions will be with us soon.

You could choose to mirror a planted border or a spread of water. Any simple surface can be made the most of with mir-rored reflections, so that elements become inseparable and dis-solve into ambiguity. As the sun hits one area, the whole space is lightened; this is especially useful in a basement area where light

△ A view that will constantly change as the planting behind you develops through the year. Slim, upright yews (*Taxus* spp.) anchor the mirror to the wall.

levels are low. By reflecting a green wall you can magnify the sense of encompassing greenery. Reflective screens angled down to mirror the floor surface can have an astonishing effect, especially if your choice of hard landscaping is something like black and white terrazzo diamonds. A stone cube placed against a mirror wall will double its apparent size and therefore its impact; an effective device in a contemporary setting.

Mirrored panels need to be recessed in a frame that itself forms an integrated part of the garden. An old door frame, for example, could be given a mirrored panel inset and incorporated snugly into its surroundings by extending the moulding along the wall or encouraging a climber to drape itself across one corner.

Solid boundaries and internal divisions can provide the surface for murals, mosaics and *trompe-l'oeil* effects to attract your attention away from disturbances. A piece of traditional statuary set against a *trompe-l'oeil* fresco in a classically styled

TROMPE-L'OEIL

LITERALLY translated as 'fooling the eye', *trompe-l'oeil* usually relies on the artifice of creating false, prolonged perspective on a flat surface. A painted image or scene with exaggerated depth can draw the eye as though down a long tunnel to a distant vanishing point. Here, the trellis battens are angled to a point on a supposed horizon, reinforcing the deceptive view past the open door. The view itself is, of course, a mirrored reflection, and a cleverly executed one, as the viewer's own reflection, when standing head on, is not caught. The result is a 'deceit' that is simple, effective and, although there is no attempt at complete realism, totally believable.

The success stems from a clever choice of materials alongside a sense of fun to bring about a touch of magic. Textures are subtly contrasted – rough plasterwork with smoother timber battens and the clean, hard glass; glossy, symmetrical evergreen wall shrubs showing off the soft, grassy tussocks on the ground. Colours are also used with a purpose – those low ornamental grasses are a softer tone of the door stain, while the punchy primrose yellow of the trellis battens really pulls the eye through the narrow gap to beyond. Not only is the part-open 'door' a natural distraction, but its suggestion of a further area of garden has the effect of emphasizing the enclosed, private atmosphere of the real garden – altogether this is a piece of compelling, lively decoration.

formal garden will appear to walk out from the wall. Such pieces of art need to be well integrated into their surroundings so that they will appear to be part of the overall fabric and yet not be completely realistic, or boredom will set in. They must be interesting enough to cause comment.

Spotlights and moonlight

The best form of lighting at night is the moon and the stars, one for the amount of light it can flood our gardens with and the other for the delight and fascination. Lighting the outside space in a magical form, with candles, flickering oil lamps and dancing spots of light, looks great, but is not always practical. Wax flares on sticks give wider spreads of light for about four hours, and sometimes this is just the right effect as long as you can clearly see your way around.

Functional lighting makes the garden safe and usable at the flick of a switch, without resorting to cold and hideous security floodlighting. This will give clarity to changes in level and access points and truly show the way.

Low-voltage lighting is safe and has the advantage of neater fittings. The power comes via the transformer, the bulky item, from the mains supply, with cable that does not need to be housed in a conduit, although you will need to know where the system runs around the garden to avoid slicing through the cable with your spade. Movable earth spikes support the fittings that clip onto the cable for uplighting. Functional and ornamental lighting sources should be kept on separate circuits for different occasions.

Unless the fitting is intended to be a feature in its own right, it should be as unobtrusive as possible; after all, it is the effect of the pool of light that matters. Small is beautiful and fittings can be neatly channelled into the side of walls, fencing, trellis and step risers to focus on specific areas and give attention to eye-catching plants and other features. Downlighters can have louvres fitted to minimize glare, appropriate for areas of high use. Filtering downlighting through overhead screening and tree canopies gives a subtle effect and brings a whole new character to screened areas. With sensitive lighting you can continue to enjoy garden areas and feel quite concealed by the enfolding darkness. Similarly, beautiful and functional effects can be given by allowing the light pool to just graze across surfaces, defining textures and highlighting any changes in level.

Spotlighting features and focal points will contribute to your sense of seclusion from beyond the boundaries. Textured and coloured tree stems look stunning when lit, especially the white stems of birch (*Betula utilis* var. *jacquemontii*), the flaky, peeling

△ A mirror will capture and reflect the movement of water even if the jet is switched off.

△ Mirrors set at angles will multiply low images.

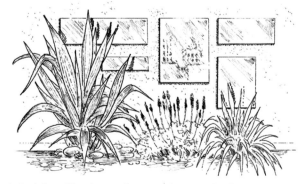

△ A plain utilitarian surface can be completely altered by the addition of an arrangement of small mirrors.

▷ The magical effects of downlighters strengthen as the natural light fades and the white-edge foliage of the hosta and the scented flowers of the confederate jasmine (*Trachelospermum jasminoides*) become almost ethereal.

stems of the paper bark maple (*Acer griseum*) and the snake bark maple (*A. davidii*), and the steely, grey stem of the snow gum (*Eucalyptus pauciflora* subsp. *niphophila*). Large specimen trees will need side beams crossing at an angle for a full effect. For a lovely, ghostly effect what could be better than uplighting a small group of trees. Pools and moving water can be backlit so that the water reflects and mirrors details; objects will glow and stand out in relief.

The focus of your garden at night might be the same as during the day but given a new, nocturnal character, or items that merge into the background by day might be brought alive at night. Even in a large rural garden, views that are special will disappear once darkness falls, but new angles of interest can come into their own, and a partially hidden container or shy piece of statuary become the night-time focus.

By introducing subtle lighting effects it is possible to cut out the world beyond and enjoy the privacy of your garden at night. 'Subtle' is the key word in this context, because it is necessary to find a happy medium where you can happily enjoy the space when darkness descends, without feeling in the spotlight.

□

A garden that tries to incorporate all these effects is likely to be a mess, with no sense of harmony or identity. It is not always easy to decide what is going to work best for you and your plot, and it can be tempting to try a bit of everything. Simplicity is often the best answer, however; if in doubt go for understatement rather than overstatement. Spend time thinking about the sort of atmosphere – romantic? exotic? contemplative? – with which you would like to imbue your new-found seclusion. Mocking up ideas, as I suggested in Chapter 1 (see page 8), will help you to gauge their effect before you commit yourself to a major expense or upheaval, but every combination of person and plot is unique and in the end the happiest and most successful solutions may be the result of serendipity.

Plant Directory

THESE categories aim to provide a quick guide to choosing the best plants for a specific purpose. Growth rate, availability, hardiness and visual effect were the chief criteria, with personal preference alongside restrictions of space in this chapter as an editing tool. Each plant entry includes the main attributes as well as other characteristics, such as perfume, seasonal interest, pollution tolerance and habit. Other relevant species or varieties are also included.

Expected height and spread at 5 and 10 years are given, except in Hedging for boundaries (page 121) and Low divisions within the garden (page 122) where planting distances and growth rate based on a 5-year span are given instead.

Symbols

E	evergreen
D	deciduous
★	pollution tolerant
NH	not winter hardy
H	tolerates a minimum temperature of -5°C (23°F)
HH	tolerates a minimum temperature of -15°C (5°F)
HHH	tolerates a minimum temperature of -18°C (0°F)
G	growth rate

Plants for overhead screening

This section includes vigorous rambling and climbing plants that will happily grow up into trees and/or cover a structure successfully after initial guidance. They need no support from companion plants and each has a strong visual effect. The Russian vine (*Fallopia baldschuanica*) and *Rosa filipes* 'Kiftsgate' are two obvious omissions, as their tremendous growth rate makes them more of a hazard than a help.

Actinidia deliciosa (syn. *A. chinensis;* Chinese gooseberry, kiwi fruit)
D ★ HH Size: 12 × 12m (39 × 39ft)
G 5 yrs: 3 × 3m (10 × 10ft);
10yrs: 6 × 6m (20 × 20ft)
Aspect: Full sun; tolerates light shade.
Soil: Any reasonable soil except waterlogged ground.
Fast-growing climber, with a vigorous twisting and twining habit. Large, coarse, curving, mid-green foliage. Needs a very sheltered site for fruit to develop.

Akebia quinata (chocolate vine)
D HH Size: 6 × 10m (20 × 33ft)
G 5 yrs: 1.8 × 1.8m (6 × 6ft);
10yrs: 6 × 6m (20 × 20ft)
Aspect: Needs some protection from midday sun and from cold winds; can be evergreen in very sheltered sites.
Soil: Any reasonable soil; copes with some alkalinity.
Twining stems support soft, waxy, divided clear green foliage. Hanging burgundy flowers in spring .

Aristolochia macrophylla (syn. *A. durior, A. sipho*; Dutchman's pipe)
D HH Size: 6 × 6m (20 × 20ft)
G 5 yrs: 1.8 × 1.5m (6 × 5ft);
10yrs: 3 × 3m (10 × 10ft)
Aspect: Sheltered conditions in light shade.
Soil: Needs good, rich, deep soil.
Large, heart-shaped, light green foliage. Pale, tubular flowers in early summer.

Campsis × tagliabuana
D ★ HH Size: 12 × 12m (39 × 39ft)
G 5 yrs: 3 × 3m (10 × 10ft);
10yrs: 6 × 6m (20 × 20ft)
Aspect: Full sun; sheltered conditions.
Soil: Needs good, rich soil, and tolerates clay.
Vigorous creeping habit, with twining stems and tendrils. Light green leaves. *C. × t.* 'Madame Galen' has orange-red, trumpet flowers, in late summer. *C. radicans* ★ (trumpet vine, trumpet honeysuckle) is a less refined substitute.

Clematis armandii
E ★ HH Size: 7 × 7m (23 × 23ft)
G 5 yrs: 3 × 3m (10 × 10ft);
10yrs: 6 × 6m (20 × 20ft)
Aspect: Needs a sheltered, sunny aspect that provides maximum warmth and light for the top growth.
Soil: Any well-drained soil.

Ranging habit, twining stems and prominent glossy foliage. Scented, pure white, waxy flowers in spring.

Clematis montana
D HH Size: 10 × 10m (33 × 33ft)
G 5 yrs: 5 × 5m (16 × 16ft);
10yrs: 8 × 8m (26 × 26ft)
Aspect: Any aspect but reduced performance in too much sun.
Soil: Good, moist loam.
Vigorous twiner. Early show of open, white flowers. *C. m.* 'Elizabeth' has more perfumed, pink flowers. *C. m.* f. *grandiflora* has larger white, unscented flowers while *C. m.* var. *rubens* has darker purple-tinged foliage and pink, vanilla-scented flowers.

Hedera canariensis (Canary Island ivy)
E ★ HH Size: 8 × 8m (26 × 26ft)
G 5 yrs: 2.1 × 2.1m (7 × 7ft);
10yrs: 4 × 4m (13 × 13ft)
Aspect: Any, but not too exposed. Variegated forms need more light.
Soil: Well-drained soil.
Partially self-clinging. Very large dark leaves have light undersides. More showy forms include *H. azorica* (syn. *H. c.* var. *azorica*), which has lighter foliage, and *H. c.* 'Gloire de Marengo', which has creamy white variegation.

Hedera colchica (Persian ivy)
E ★ HH Size: 8 × 8m (26 × 26ft)
G 5 yrs: 2.1 × 2.1m (7 × 7ft);
10yrs: 4 × 4m (13 × 13ft)
Aspect: Any but prefers light shade.
Soil: Well-drained soil, including clay.
Climbing habit and partially self-clinging. Dark, matt green heart-shaped leaves. Variegated forms include *H. c.* 'Dentata Variegata' (yellow margins) and *H. c.* 'Sulphur Heart' (syn. *H. c.* 'Paddy's Pride') (central yellow splash and veined pattern).

Hydrangea anomala subsp. petiolaris
(syn. *H. petiolaris*, *H. tiliifolia*; climbing hydrangea)
D ★ HH Size: 12 × 12m (39 × 39ft)
G 5 yrs: 2.1 × 2.1m (7 × 7ft);
10yrs: 6 × 6m (20 × 20ft)
Aspect: Tolerates partial shade.
Soil: Fertile, reasonably retentive soil; tolerates clay.
Vigorous climber, clinging by aerial roots. Rich green foliage supports large, flat, lacecap flowers in summer. *Schizophragma*

hydrangeoides (Japanese hydrangea vine) is similar, but more showy and less vigorous.

Jasminum officinale (common white jasmine)
D ★ HH Height: 10m (33ft)
G 5 yrs: 4 × 4m (13 × 13ft);
10yrs: 8 × 8m (26 × 26ft)
Aspect: Any, but not too exposed; semi-evergreen in warm, sheltered sites.
Soil: Any.
Fast-growing with pretty, mid-green foliage and fragrant star flowers.

Lonicera japonica 'Halliana' (Japanese honeysuckle)
E HH Size: 9 × 9m (30 × 30ft)
G 5 yrs: 3 × 3m (10 × 10ft);
10yrs: 6 × 6m (20 × 20ft)
Aspect: Reasonable light.
Soil: Good, rich soil.
Rambling habit, fresh green foliage and a long display of fragrant, creamy yellow flowers. Evergreen *L. henryi* ★ is less spectacular.

Parthenocissus quinquefolia (syn. Vitis quinquefolia; virginia creeper, five-leaved ivy)
D ★ HHH Size: 10 × 10m (33 × 33ft)
G 5 yrs: 3 × 3m (10 × 10ft);
10 yrs: 5 × 5m (16 × 16ft)
Aspect: Full sun, tolerates light shade.
Soil: Deep, fertile soil.
Layered foliage is striking in autumn. Alternatively, use *P. henryana* (see page 120) and *P. tricuspidata* (see page 124).

Rosa 'Albertine'
D ★ HH Size: 5 × 5m (16 × 16ft)
G 5 yrs: 3 × 3m (10 × 10ft);
10yrs: 5 × 5m (16 × 16ft)
Aspect: Light shade to full sun.
Soil: Good, fertile soil.
Vigorous, with a good framework but vicious thorns. Fleshy, apricot pink, strongly fragrant blooms all summer. *R.* 'New Dawn', with silver-pink, fragrant flowers, is less vigorous and dislikes shade. *R.* 'Brenda Colvin' makes a larger plant.

Rosa 'Wedding Day'
D ★ HHH Size: 9 × 6m (30 × 20ft)
G 5 yrs: 6 × 3m (20 × 10ft);
10yrs: 9 × 6m (30 × 20ft)
Aspect: Full sun to medium shade.
Soil: Good, deep rich soil.

Vigorous climber which has clusters of shell white, fragrant single blooms in mid-summer. *R.* 'Rambling Rector', *R.* 'Albéric Barbier' and *R.* 'Bobbie James' all have white flowers. *R.* 'Paul's Himalayan Musk', similar in habit to *R.* 'Wedding Day', has shell pink flowers.

Vitis 'Brant' (vine)
D HH Size: 9 × 9m (30 × 30ft)
G 5 yrs: 3 × 3m (10 × 10ft);
10yrs: 6 × 6m (20 × 20ft)
Aspect: Full sun to light shade.
Soil: Many, best in good, deep, loam.
Needs initial support. Large foliage, changing colour fast in late summer, when grapes appear. A fruiting vine if pruned carefully.

Vitis coignetiae (crimson glory vine)
D HH Size: 12 × 12m (39 × 39ft)
G 5 yrs: 4 × 4m (13 × 13ft);
10yrs: 10 × 10m (33 × 33ft)
Aspect: Average; best in light shade.
Soil: Good, deep, fertile and moisture-retentive but not waterlogged. Tolerates clay.
Vigorous but needs initial support. Coarse, large, dark green leaves; excellent autumn colour.

Vitis vinifera 'Purpurea' (Tenturier vine)
D HH Size: 7 × 7m (23 × 23ft)
G 5 yrs: 3 × 3m (10 × 10ft);
10yrs: 5 × 5m (16 × 16ft)
Aspect: Full sun; tolerates light shade.
Soil: Deep, fertile, moisture-retentive.
Claret red leaves changing to scarlet and dark reddish-purple.

Wisteria floribunda (Japanese wisteria)
D H Size: 9 × 9m (30 × 30ft)
G 5 yrs: 3 × 3m (10 × 10ft);
10yrs: 6 × 6m (20 × 20ft)
Aspect: Warm, sheltered conditions.
Soil: Good, deep root run in moisture-retentive soil.
Fresh foliage, yellow in autumn, on twining stems. Flowers, in long racemes in early summer: varieties give white, violets, mauves or pinks. Larger *W. f.* 'Multijuga' (syn. *W. f.* 'Macrobotrys') has vanilla-scented racemes up to 90cm (3ft) long. *W. sinensis* (Chinese wisteria) is more vigorous; its many hybrids have scented deep purple, chalky mauves, pinks or pure white flowers.

Plants for clothing walls and pillars

These are shrubs and less invasive climbers that can dress or cover up boundary screens and free-standing walls. They can act as soft dressing for arbours, arches and garden buildings, where their special characteristics – perfume, seasonal effect and tactile qualities – will be evident.

Arbutus unedo (strawberry tree)
E ★ H Size: 6 × 6m (20 × 20ft)
G 5 yrs: 2.1 × 2.1m (7 × 7ft);
10yrs: 4 × 4m (13 × 13ft)
Aspect: Sheltered light shade in mild, damp situations.
Soil: Any; prefers neutral to acid soil.
Foliage is tough and dark. White or pink autumn flowers are followed by round, red 'strawberry' fruits.

Azara microphylla
E H Size: 6 × 4m (20 × 13ft)
G 5 yrs: 2.1 × 1.5m (7 × 5ft);
10yrs: 4 × 3m (13 × 10ft)
Aspect: Shelter, full sun to light shade.
Soil: Well-drained: resents extremes of dry and damp.
Slow to establish. Small, dark green leaves and tiny strongly scented yellow flowers, in late winter to early spring.

Carpenteria californica
E H Size: 3 × 3m (10 × 10ft)
G 5 yrs: 1.5 × 1.5m (5 × 5ft);
10yrs: 2.1 × 2.1m (7 × 7ft)
Aspect: Sheltered full sun.
Soil: Moist, well-drained soil.
Glossy dark foliage, and fragrant, yellow-centred white flowers in summer.

Ceanothus 'Autumnal Blue'
E HH Size: 5 × 5m (16 × 16ft)
G 5 yrs: 3 × 3m (10 × 10ft);
10yrs: 4 × 4m (13 × 13ft)
Aspect: Full sun, sheltered from wind.
Soil: Deep, rich, well-drained soil.
Fast-growing, it must be fixed firmly to a support. Glossy foliage, with panicles of mid-blue flowers in late summer. One of the hardiest Ceanothus, as are C. 'A.T. Johnson' (light blue flowers in late spring), C. × veitchianus (dark blue flowers in spring and again in late summer), C. impressus (very small, curled dark leaves and deep blue summer flowers) and C. × delileanus 'Gloire de Versailles' ★ (deciduous, with soft, powdery blue flowers through summer).

Chaenomeles speciosa (quince)
D ★ HHH Size: 4 × 4m (13 × 13ft)
G 5 yrs: 2.1 × 2.1m (7 × 7ft);
10yrs: 4 × 4m (13 × 13ft)
Aspect: Full sun or deep shade
Soil: Any reasonable soil.
Flowers appear on bare stems in spring, followed by foliage and then yellow, edible fruits, which ripen in autumn. C. s. 'Nivalis' has pure white flowers. C. × superba is not quite as vigorous. C. × s. 'Rowallane' bears blood red flowers.

Clematis cirrhosa
E HH Size: 4 × 4m (13 × 13ft)
G 5 yrs: 2.1 × 2.1m (7 × 7ft);
10yrs: 3 × 3m (10 × 10ft)
Aspect: Shelter from strong winds; roots in shade and head in sun.
Soil: Reasonably moist soil.
Deep, green ferny foliage and an early show of buttery yellow bells.

Clematis, large-flowered hybrids
D HH Size: 5 × 5m (16 × 16ft)
G 5 yrs: 3 × 3m (10 × 10ft);
10yrs: 4 × 4m (13 × 13ft)
Aspect: Roots in shade, head in full sun.
Soil: Good, loamy soil with adequate moisture.
A wide choice of forms include C. 'Marie Boisselot' (white flowers from early to late summer), C. 'Niobe' (velvety dark red flowers; tolerates all aspects) and C. 'The President' (medium-sized purple flowers intermittently through summer; tolerates most aspects, but not extremes).

Cytisus battandieri (Moroccan broom, pineapple broom)
D HH Size: 6 × 6m (20 × 20ft)
G 5 yrs: 4 × 4m (13 × 13ft);
10yrs: 5 × 5m (16 × 16ft)
Aspect: Warm, sheltered position.
Soil: Any, but best on neutral, well-drained loam.
Initially fast growing. Silky, silver leaves and bright yellow pineapple-scented flowering spikes in midsummer. Fremontodendron californicum, an evergreen, has more strident flower colour but is unscented.

× Fatshedera lizei (tree ivy)
E ★ HH Size: 6 × 4m (20 × 13ft)
G 5 yrs: 2.1 × 2.1m (7 × 7ft);
10yrs: 4 × 4m (13 × 13ft)
Aspect: Sheltered shade, tolerates sun.
Soil: Deep root run in moist soil.
Needs support for upward growth. Leaves are large and shiny. Variegated forms are less hardy.

Fatsia japonica (syn. Aralia sieboldii; Japanese aralia)
E ★ HH Size: 5 × 5m (16 × 16ft)
G 5 yrs: 3 × 3m (10 × 10ft);
10yrs: 4 × 4m (13 × 13ft)
Aspect: Warm sheltered site in deep shade.
Soil: Deep, rich soil.
Dramatic, glossy foliage like large hands. Perfect for adverse urban conditions.

Ficus carica (fig)
D HH Size: 6 × 6m (20 × 20ft)
G 5 yrs: 3 × 3m (10 × 10ft);
10yrs: 5 × 5m (16 × 16ft)
Aspect: Against a warm, protected wall.
Soil: Any well-drained soil.
Handsome, veined foliage creates strong shade patterns. Constrict roots in a sunken container to encourage fruiting.

Garrya elliptica (silk tassel bush)
E ★ HH Size: 5 × 5m (16 × 16ft)
G 5 yrs: 2.1 × 2.1m (7 × 7ft);
10yrs: 3 × 3m (10 × 10ft)
Aspect: Sun or light shade; needs shelter.
Soil: Any well-drained soil.
Bushy, fast-growing plant has dark, glossy foliage with upward-thrusting stems and flower catkins. Long, drooping silvery green tassels in winter. Itea illicifolia has similar habit and foliage, but produces its even longer catkins in summer.

Hedera helix 'Oro di Bogliasco'
(syn. H. h. 'Goldheart')
E ★ HHH Size: 8 × 6m (26 × 20ft)
G 5 yrs: 4 × 2.1m (13 × 7ft);
10yrs: 6 × 4m (20 × 13ft)
Aspect: Any. Yellow forms need much light but full sun can cause scorching.
Soil: Any reasonable moist soil.
After initial help, it is tidy in habit, with small regular pointed leaves and irregular coloration. H. h. 'Buttercup' is bright yellow, turning to green in shade. H. h. 'Caecilia' (syn. H. h. 'Clotted Cream') is softer in tone. H. h. 'Parsley Crested' (syn. H. h. 'Cristata') has curling, rounded foliage with crinkly edges.

Jasminum nudiflorum (winter jasmine)
D HH Size: 4 × 5m (13 × 16ft)
G 5yrs: 2.1 × 2.1m (7 × 7ft);
10yrs: 4 × 4m (13 × 13ft)
Aspect: Any
Soil: Any
Clear yellow, star-like flowers on dark, green, slender stems through winter. Strong green foliage the rest of the year. It will need fixing to supporting wires.

Lonicera periclymenum (woodbine, common honeysuckle)
D HH Size: 6 × 6m (20 × 20ft)
G 5 yrs: 2.1 × 2.1m (7 × 7ft);
10yrs: 4 × 4m (13 × 13ft)
Aspect: Tolerates most sheltered aspects but prefers to have its roots shaded.
Soil: Deep, rich, moist loam.
Twining, fast-growing climber with highly fragrant blossoms. *L. p.* 'Belgica' (early Dutch woodbine) has pink and cream flowers in early summer, more fragrant in the evening. More attractive and similarly scented, *L. p.* 'Serotina' (late Dutch honeysuckle) has darker foliage and flowers from midsummer on. *L. p.* 'Graham Thomas' has scented, yellow blossoms throughout summer. Unscented *L. × tellmanniana* has coppery orange flowers, brushed with a red stain. *L. tragophylla*, a true rambler, best in light shade, produces yellow, tubular blossoms.

Magnolia grandiflora (bull bay, southern magnolia)
E ★ HH Size: 8 × 8m (26 × 26ft)
G 5 yrs: 1.8 × 1.8m (6 × 6ft); 10yrs:
4 × 4m (13 × 13ft)
Aspect: Sheltered position against a tall wall in full sun to light shade.
Soil: Most soils, including alkaline with enough good top soil.
Glossy dark green leaves and huge, scented, waxy flowers in summer.

Parthenocissus henryana (syn. *Ampelopsis henryana*; *Vitis henryana*; Chinese virginia creeper)
D ★ HHH Size: 8 × 8m (26 × 26ft)
G 5 yrs: 1.8 × 1.8m (6 × 6ft);
10yrs: 4 × 4m (13 × 13ft)
Aspect: Best in light shade: strong sun can destroy the variegated effect.
Soil: Any deep, moist loamy soil.
Vigorous climber, clinging with adhesive pads. Silver-veined, dark green palmate leaves. Colour develops from burgundy to scarlet through autumn. *P. tricuspidata* is described in Plants to use as Focal Points (see page 124) for its autumn colour.

Passiflora caerulea (syn. *P. chinensis*, *P. mayana*; common passion flower)
D H Size: 8 × 8m (26 × 26ft)
G 5 yrs: 2.4 × 2.4m (8 × 8ft);
10yrs: 6 × 6m (20 × 20ft)
Aspect: Full sun or very light shade in a sheltered position.
Soil: Any well-drained, even poor, soil.
Mid-green, divided foliage and ivory white flowers with central threads of blue in summer. Oval fruits after a long, hot summer.

Pileostegia viburnoides (syn. *Schizophragma viburnoides*; climbing viburnum)
E HH Size: 6 × 6m (20 × 20ft)
G 5 yrs: 1.5 × 1.5m (5 × 5ft);
10yrs: 3 × 3m (10 × 10ft)
Aspect: Any, but not too exposed.
Soil: Any adequately moist soil.
Slow-growing, with clinging aerial roots. Long, pointed, leathery leaves and delicate cream flowers in late summer.

Piptanthus nepalensis (syn. *P. forrestii*, *P. laburnifolius*; evergreen laburnum)
E HH Size: 4 × 3m (13 × 10ft)
G 5 yrs: 2.1 × 1.5m (7 × 5ft);
10yrs: 3 × 2.4m (10 × 8ft)
Aspect: Most, except deep shade.
Soil: Well-drained soil.
Stiff, upright bottlebrush effect with bright yellow, pea-flowers in late spring.

Prunus 'Morello' (acid cherry)
D HH Size: 4 × 5m (13 × 16ft)
G 5 yrs: 2.1 × 2.1m (7 × 7ft);
10yrs: 4 × 4m (13 × 13ft)
Aspect: Tolerates light shade; needs shelter of a light screen.
Soil: Any that is not waterlogged.
White flowers in spring before foliage. Dark red fruits in late summer; cover with netting to protect from birds. Good autumn colour. Tie to wire to fan-train.

Pyracantha 'Mohave'
E ★ HH Size: 4 × 3m (13 × 10ft)
G 5 yrs: 2.1 × 1.5m (7 × 5ft);
10yrs: 4 × 2.1m (13 × 7ft)
Aspect: Any except deep shade.
Soil: Most neutral soils.
Vigorous thorny shrub. Strong green foliage, white summer flowers and many orange-red berries. Tie in to maintain horizontal tiers. *P.* 'Golden Charmer' is similar in form with yellow berries.

Roses, climbing
D HH Size: 5 × 5m (16 × 16ft)
G 5 yrs: 3 × 3 (10 × 10ft);
10 yrs 5 × 5m (16 × 16ft)
Aspect: Prefer full sun to light shade.
Soil: Good, rich soil.
Rosa 'Aloha' has dark foliage and pink blooms from late spring to late summer. *R.* 'Climbing Sombreuil' (syn. *R.* 'Colonial White') is less vigorous with rounded pure white blossoms. *R.* 'Dublin Bay' shows scented, crimson blooms throughout summer. *R.* 'Leverkusen' has a continuous display of soft, creamy yellow blossoms. *R.* 'Maigold' has spasmodic coppery flowers. Elegant *R.* 'Meg' has dark, glossy foliage and scented, apricot blooms. Double-flowered *R.* 'Parade' is a good pillar rose, with perfumed, crimson blooms. *R.* 'Paul's Perpetual White' has large, single, off-white flowers. *R.* 'Paul's Scarlet Climber' bears clusters of bright red, double flowers. Continual-flowering *R.* 'Phyllis Bide' has blooms tinged pink, salmon and gold.

Solanum crispum 'Glasnevin' (Chilean potato tree)
E HH Size: 4 × 4m (13 × 13ft)
G 5 yrs: 2.1 × 2.1m (7 × 7ft);
10yrs: 3 × 3m (10 × 10ft)
Aspect: Full sun or light shade; semi-evergreen in a warm, sheltered position.
Soil: Most soils, but not extremes.
Long, flexible stems need controlling. Leaves are narrow and pointed, and clusters of purple-blue flowers appear over a long period. The semi-evergreen *S. jasminoides* 'Album' (potato vine) has white flowers.

Trachelospermum jasminoides (confederate jasmine, star jasmine)
E H Size: 4 × 4m.13 × 13ft)
G 5 yrs: 1.5 × 1.5m (5 × 5ft);
10yrs: 3 × 3m (10 × 10ft)
Aspect: Full sun to light shade in a warm sheltered position.
Soil: Prefers a moist root run in neutral soil.
Fragrant slow-starter. Mid-green oval leaves, and clusters of waxy, white flowers through the summer. Tie in to wires to encourage upward growth.

Vitis vinifera 'Incana' (vine)
D HH Size: 5 × 5m (16 × 16ft)
G 5 yrs: 3 × 3m (10 × 10ft);
10yrs: 5 × 5m (16 × 16ft)
Aspect: Sheltered position in full sun or light shade.
Soil: Deep, fertile, moisture-retentive soil.
Silvery, felted foliage through the summer.

Hedging for boundaries

The plants suggested here will form an obvious and, in certain cases, a dense, impenetrable barrier. They could be planted to establish a formal hedge that would require clipping or they could be left to spread and integrate with their neighbours at will. The planting distance is indicated as well as the expected average height after 5 years.

Evergreen hedging

Berberis darwinii
E ★ HHH Average height: 1.5m (5ft); will easily reach 2.4m (8ft) if required
Planting distance: 60cm (2ft)
Aspect: Full sun or light shade.
Soil: Any soil.
Small foliage and some spines create a dense, thicket barrier. Orange flowers in spring and purple berries in autumn. Prune after flowering, or leave for an informal effect. *B. gagnepainii* var. *lanceifolia* has more spines and yellow flowers. *B.* × *stenophylla* has an arching habit and brilliant yellow flowers in spring. *B. sargentiana* has tougher leathery foliage and yellow flowers.

Buxus sempervirens (box)
E ★ HHH Average height: 60cm (2ft)
Planting distance: 30cm (1ft)
Aspect: Shade tolerant.
Soil: Any.
Small, glossy leaves are dense and aromatic. Slow to start. Trim in spring or late summer to keep formal shapes.

Cotoneaster lacteus
E HHH Average height: 1.5m (5ft)
Planting distance: 60cm (2ft) or more
Aspect: Full sun or light shade.
Soil: Any good soil.
This forms a dense barrier. Dark green leaves, white flowers then red berries lasting through autumn and winter. Prune lightly after flowering or clip severely into a more structured form. *C. simonsii* is more

arching; treat less severely for informal habit.

Elaeagnus × *ebbingei*
E ★ HH Average height: 1.2m (4ft)
Planting distance: 60cm (2ft)
Aspect: Full sun to mid shade, good for coastal situations.
Soil: Any soil.
Large, tough, oval silvery leaves. Clip heavily or allow to thicken naturally. *E. pungens*, which has good, glossy foliage, grows in an angular, more obviously branching fashion.

Escallonia rubra var. *macrantha*
E ★ HH Average height: 1.2m (4ft)
Planting distance: 60cm (2ft)
Aspect: Full sun to light shade. Coastal situations.
Soil: Any soil.
Semi-formal, dense, rambling habit. Glossy dark green foliage and rosy red flowers. Prune after first flowering to encourage second flush. *E. r.* 'Crimson Spire' has bright crimson flowers.

Euonymus japonicus
E ★ H Average height: 90 cm (3ft)
Planting distance: 45cm (18in
Aspect: Tolerates shade and coastal sites.
Soil: Any.
Susceptible to frost damage. Glossy, elliptical foliage stands proud. *Griselinia littoralis* has similar characteristics.

Ilex aquifolium (common holly)
E ★ HHH Average height: 1.2m (4ft)
Planting distance: 45cm (18in)
Aspect: Shade-tolerant.
Soil: Any soil.
Handsome, dark green foliage creates a dense, spiny barrier. Either keep clipped or leave in a laxer habit. Female plant berries in winter where both sexes are present. *I.* × *altaclarensis* (Highclere holly) has larger, less spiny leaves.

Ligustrum ovalifolium (twiggy privet, oval-leaved privet)
E ★ HHH Average height: 1.8m (6ft)
Planting distance: 30cm (1ft)
Aspect: Shade-tolerant.
Soil: Tolerates poor soil.
Makes a neat screen. Small, oval leaves can be kept tightly clipped (as normally seen) or, if there is sufficient space, left to thicken in a more natural habit.

Prunus laurocerasus (cherry laurel, common laurel)
E ★ HHH Average height: 1.5m (5ft)
Planting distance: 60cm (2ft)
Aspect: Shade-tolerant.
Soil: Any well-drained soil.
Deep green, glossy foliage and a thick stem system make a heavy hedge, needing space. Prune in summer. *P. l.* 'Otto Luyken', better for more compact settings, is an upright form with narrower, pointed leaves. *P. lusitanica* (Portuguese laurel) has darker foliage and a more accommodating habit. *Aucuba japonica* ★ (spotted laurel) is an acceptable substitute.

Taxus baccata (yew)
E ★ HHH Average height: 1.2m (4ft)
Planting distance: 45cm (18in)
Aspect: Shade-tolerant.
Soil: Any well-drained soil.
One of the best conifer hedges. Feed and trim to encourage more rapid growth. Trim in late summer.

Thuja plicata 'Atrovirens' (western red cedar)
E HH Average height: 1.5m (5ft); taller in sheltered sites
Planting distance: 60cm (2ft)
Aspect: Tolerates light shade.
Soil: Most soils, but not waterlogged.
Good, dense, fresh green conifer, aromatic and trouble free. Grows fast, even when established plants are used. Clip back in summer.

Viburnum tinus (laurustinus)
E ★ HH Average height: 1.5m (5ft); taller in sheltered sites
Planting distance: 60cm (2ft)
Aspect: Sun; shelter from cold winds.
Soil: Any well-drained soil.
Very dense shrub with attractive habit. Flowers are freely borne in sun: pink buds opening to white flowers from late autumn to spring. The good, tough foliage makes a sound hedge.

Deciduous hedging

Berberis thunbergii f. *atropurpurea*
D ★ HHH Average height: 1.5m (5ft) or more
Planting distance: 60cm (2ft)
Aspect: Sun
Soil: Any reasonably moist soil.

Upright thorny shrub makes a daunting but attractive screen. Small, rounded, copper-purple foliage intensifies in autumn. Red fruits. Trim in winter.

Carpinus betulus (common hornbeam)
D ★ HHH Average height: 1.5m (5ft)
Planting distance: 45cm (18in
Aspect: Sun to light shade. Withstands exposed sites.
Soil: Clay and chalk soils.
Oval, grey-green foliage and twiggy stems make a good barrier. Autumn leaves turn paper-bag brown, and some are retained well into winter. Stagger plants for a more effective barrier.

Crataegus monogyna (common hawthorn, may)
D ★ HHH Average height: 1.2m (4ft)
Planting distance: 30cm (1ft)
Aspect: Light shade, tolerates exposure.
Soil: Any reasonable soil.
Tangled, dense framework eventually makes an impenetrable hedge. White scented flowers and red, autumn fruits.

Fagus sylvatica (beech)
D HHH Average height: 1.5m (5ft)
Planting distance: 45cm (18in
Aspect: Prefers sun.
Soil: Tolerates chalky soils.
Large, oval leaves on a twiggy structure. Fresh, green, spring growth deepens in summer before turning golden-brown in autumn. Plant individual beeches in a staggered formation to create a more obvious barrier from the start.

Hippophae rhamnoides (sea buckthorn)
D HH Average height: 1.8m (6ft)
Planting distance: 80cm (32in) or more
Aspect: Best in sun; good in coastal sites.
Soil: Light soil; can cope with most soils.
Forms a very spiny barrier. Narrow metallic grey leaves, and strongly coloured orange berries in autumn and winter if male and female plants are mixed. Trim in spring. Needs space.

Rosa rugosa
D ★ HHH Average height: 1.2m (4ft)
Planting distance: 45cm (18in
Aspect: Full sun or very light shade; tolerates coastal conditions.
Soil: Any moist, fertile soil.
Vigorous, prickly plant is ideal for dense hedging. Fresh green leaves, wide range of pink and red flowers, and hips with yellow autumn foliage. R. r. 'Alba' flowers late: brilliant contrast between white blooms and huge, red hips. R. 'Roseraie de l'Haÿ' has strongly scented, large, loose, crimson-purple blooms. The following make a reasonably good barrier with some ornamental interest: Rosa pimpinellifolia (syn. R. spinosissima; burnet rose, Scotch rose) (white, single flowers); R. 'Stanwell Perpetual' (arching with recurrent double, fragrant, pink-white blooms); R. 'Frühlingsgold' (large golden-yellow flowers) and R. 'Frühlingszauber' (single, silver-pink flowers and dark foliage).

Low divisions within the garden

These ornamental shrubs, mostly evergreen, provide interest with scent and colour, but also discreetly split space. Many are tactile and undemanding.

Choisya ternata (Mexican orange blossom)
E ★ HH Average height: 1.2m (4ft)
Planting distance: 80cm (32in)
Aspect: Sun or shade.
Soil: Most, except not too alkaline.
Glossy leaves and very fragrant, waxy flowers in spring and summer. Some pruning needed but do not overdo and destroy its rounded habit.

Hebe 'Marjorie'
E ★ H Average height: 90cm (3ft)
Planting distance: 60cm (2ft)
Aspect: Full sun, sheltered from cold winds.
Soil: Tolerates most; prefers light soil.
Dense, rounded foliage with lilac-blue flowering spikes in midsummer. Reliable low hedge. H. 'Mrs E. Tennant' is a good substitute. H. 'Autumn Glory' is longer flowering but smaller.

Lavandula angustifolia (syn. L. officinalis, L. vera; old English lavender)
E HH Average height: 60cm (2ft)
Planting distance: 45cm (18in)
Aspect: Full sun.
Soil: Any well-drained soil.
Aromatic tufty grey-green foliage, scented flower spikes through summer. Trim in spring to prevent it becoming woody. L. a. 'Hidcote' is compact with deep, violet-blue flowers. L. a. 'Alba' has white spikes on tall stems. L. stoechas (French lavender) needs shelter, but has the bonus of showy flowers.

Osmanthus heterophyllus (syn. O. ilicifolius)
E ★ HH Average height: 90cm (3ft)
Planting distance: 60cm (2ft)
Apect: Prefers light shade, tolerates sun.
Soil: Most well-drained soils.
Dark, glossy, holly-like foliage; scented, white flowers from late summer. Dense habit, but slow to form a screen.

Rosmarinus officinalis (rosemary)
E HH Average height: 90cm (3ft)
Planting distance: 60cm (2ft)
Aspect: Full sun or very light shade.
Soil: Any light, well-drained soil.
Easy-going habit, with aromatic, grey-green foliage and blue flowers in late spring to early summer. Trim back before flowering. R. o. 'Sissinghurst Blue' and R. o. 'Benenden Blue' are good for sheltered settings.

Santolina pinnata subsp. **neapolitana** (syn. S. tomentosa)
E HH Average height: 50cm (20in)
Planting distance: 30cm (1ft)
Aspect: Full sun.
Soil: Any open, well-drained soil.
Soft, grey-green, slightly aromatic foliage. Bright yellow, button flowers through summer. Trim lightly in spring.

Sarcococca confusa
E ★ HH Average height: 90cm (3ft)
Planting distance: 45cm (18in)
Aspect: Full sun to light shade.
Soil: Good, fertile soil.
Small, bushy shrub with glossy, dark green, pointed foliage. Fragrant flowers followed by black berries in winter.

Fast-growing trees for screening

These trees have clean stems that do not take up valuable space, and even in winter add a twiggy framework suitable for light screening. Pleaching trees adds height and allows more light into the garden.

Acer saccharinum (silver maple)
D ★ HHH Size: 7 × 6m (23 × 20ft)
G 5 yrs: 4 × 3m (13 × 10ft);
10yrs: 5 × 4m (16 × 13ft)
Aspect: Full sun to light shade.
Soil: Any soil.

Substantial, fast-growing tree (allow sufficient space for ultimate size) with deeply cut foliage, silvery white underneath. Yellow autumn colour.

Eucalyptus pauciflora subsp. *niphophila* (snow gum)
E ★ H Size: 10 × 4m (33 × 13ft)
G 5 yrs: 4 × 1.8m (13 × 6ft);
10yrs: 8 × 3m (26 × 10ft)
Aspect: Full sun in a sheltered situation.
Soil: Light, well-drained soil.
Less vigorous than some eucalyptuses, it is still a suitable screen; could be pollarded. Long, curving grey-green leaves and patchwork trunk.

Gleditsia triacanthos 'Sunburst' (honey locust)
D ★ HH Size: 8 × 4m (26 × 13ft)
G 5 yrs: 3 × 1.8m (10 × 6ft);
10yrs: 6 × 4m (20 × 13ft)
Aspect: Full sun or light shade.
Soil: Well-drained, deep, fertile soil.
Allow sufficient space. Angular, spiny framework, golden-yellow foliage from early summer. Prune to keep shape.

Malus hupehensis (Hupeh crab)
D ★ HHH Size: 6 × 4m (20 × 13ft)
G 5 yrs: 3 × 1.5m (10 × 5ft);
10yrs: 5 × 3m (16 × 10ft)
Aspect: Any except deep shade; prefers full sun.
Soil: Most soils but not waterlogged.
Upright habit. Fresh green foliage; fragrant white, blossom in early summer, followed by red-flushed pale fruits. *M. floribunda* (Japanese crab) has a spreading canopy. *M. transitoria* also has an umbrella with feathery leaves and yellow and red fruits.

Populus tremula (aspen)
D ★ HH Size: 8 × 4m (26 × 13ft)
G 5 yrs: 1.8 × 1m (6 × 3ft);
10yrs: 4 × 1.8m (13 × 6ft)
Aspect: Full sun, not too exposed.
Soil: Any soil but not extremes.
Whippy growth topped with small, fresh green foliage. *P. balsamifera* (balsam poplar, tacamahac, hackmatack) and *P. × candicans* are larger trees with scented foliage. *Alnus cordata* (Italian alder), with catkins and dark fruits in winter, relishes damp soil.

Sorbus vilmorinii (Vilmorin's rowan)
D ★ HHH Size: 6 × 3m (20 × 10ft)

G 5 yrs: 3 × 1.5m (10 × 5ft);
10yrs: 6 × 3m (20 × 10ft)
Aspect: Sun or light shade; tolerates exposure.
Soil: Any fertile soil.
Fast-growing, accepts close planting. Metallic grey foliage and white flowers, followed by pink-mauve berries in late summer. Similar *S. cashmiriana* (Kashmir rowan) and *S. hupehensis* (Hupeh rowan) have white berries. *S. sargentiana* (Sargent's rowan) and *S. aucuparia* (mountain ash, rowan) make slightly larger trees with orange fruiting berries and strong autumn colour.

Tilia × euchlora (Caucasian lime, Crimean lime)
D ★ HHH Size: 6 × 3m (20 × 10ft)
G 5 yrs: should reach above.
Aspect: Needs some shelter.
Soil: Any fertile soil.
Yellow shoots, glossy foliage and fragrant flowers. Adapt for a limited space by pleaching into a framework 9 months after planting. Prune back laterals to 2–3 buds in the second year; prune lightly annually thereafter. Remove framework when side branches have intermingled.

Pliable shrubs and small trees for training

Planted overhead screens need young trees or shrubs with stems that root quickly. Ultimate size is less important for these trained trees, so only the growth rate is given.

Cercis siliquastrum (Judas tree)
D ★ HHH
G 5 yrs: should reach 3 × 3m (10 × 10ft)
Aspect: Prefers light shade, sheltered position.
Soil: Neutral to acid; nurture on alkaline soil.
Good for training: twiggy habit disguises tying in. Small, kidney-shaped leaves, yellow in autumn and rose-purple flowers in early summer.

Cotoneaster frigidus 'Cornubia' (tree cotoneaster)
E ★ HH
G 5 yrs: 4 × 1.5m (13 × 5ft);
10yrs: 5 × 3m (16 × 10ft)
Aspect: Full sun to medium shade; sheltered position.

Soil: Any, particularly alkaline.
Year-round screening: espalier-train on to posts and wires. Leathery, pointed foliage and white flowers in early summer, followed by small, red fruits in late summer and autumn. *C. salicifolius* 'Pendulus' is a suitable substitute.

Malus 'John Downie' (crab apple)
D ★ HH
G 5 yrs: should reach 4 × 4m (13 × 13ft)
Aspect: Full sun to light shade; shelter.
Soil: Any soil, except waterlogged.
Fresh, green foliage, and shiny, scarlet-orange fruits in late summer and autumn. Needs sturdy framework for espalier, fan-training or training over arch. Allow for hanging fruit and foliage. Remove all side shoots back to two junctions from previous year's growth. *M. × zumi* 'Golden Hornet' (syn. *M.* 'Golden Hornet') has white flowers before bright, yellow fruits; this is a universal pollinator: can be used with *M. pumila* (apple hybrids) for good crops.

Sorbus aria (whitebeam)
D ★ HH
G 5 yrs: 3 × 3m (10 × 10ft); potentially much larger
Aspect: Full sun and some shelter (if over a structure)
Soil: Tolerates any; prefers alkaline.
Conical habit. Dark stems, silvery foliage, and white flowers in late spring. Some orange berries.

Focal point plants

Using plants to attract attention away from eyesores or intrusive elements is explored in Chapter 6. This mixed bag is by no means definitive, but my object has been to provide a 'taster' or two under each heading in more detail and alternatives for further investigation.

Striking stems

Prunus serrula (birch bark tree)
D ★ HHH Size: 8 × 4m (26 × 13ft)
G 5 yrs: 4 × 1.8m (13 × 6ft);
10yrs: 6 × 3m (20 × 10ft)
Aspect: Full sun or light shade; light must be strong in winter.
Soil: Any soil.
Trunk is shiny red-brown; outside skin peels off in long, papery strips on shady side. Fragile blossom in spring.

Alternatives for interesting bark: *Acer capillipes* (snake bark maple), *A. griseum* (paper bark maple), *A. pennsylvanicum* (striped maple); *Arbutus* × *andrachnoides* ★; *Betula utilis* var. *jacquemontii*; *Eucalyptus pauciflora* subsp. *niphophila* (snow gum) ★

Alternatives for coloured stems: *Acer palmatum* 'Sango-kaku'; *Cornus alba* 'Kesselringii', *C. a.* 'Sibirica', *C. stolonifera* 'Flaviramea'; *Rubus cockburnianus* ★; *Salix alba* subsp. *vitellina* 'Britzensis'

Colour explosions

Parthenocissus tricuspidata 'Veitchii'
(syn. *Ampelopsis tricuspidata* 'Veitchii'; Boston ivy)
D ★ HH Size: 9 × 9m (30 × 30ft)
G 5 yrs: 1.8 × 1.8m (6 × 6ft);
10yrs: 4.3 × 4.3m (14 × 14ft)
Aspect: Full sun to light shade.
Soil: Any fertile soil.
Self-clinging climber with purple-bronze foliage, brilliant blood red in autumn.

Alternatives: *Actinidia kolomikta* ★; *Amelanchier lamarckii* ★; *Canna* 'Wyoming'; *Cotinus* 'Flame'; *Dahlia* 'Bishop of Llandaff'; *Humulus lupulus* 'Aureus' (golden-leaved hop); *Nandina domestica* 'Fire Power'; *Parthenocissus quinquefolia* (virginia creeper; see page 118); *Rhus typhina*; *Rosa* 'Eye Paint' ★; *Sedum telephium* 'Matrona' (syn. S. 'Matrona'); *Sorbus commixta* 'Embley' ★

Graceful stars and spikes

Cortaderia selloana 'Pumila' (dwarf pampas grass)
E HH Size: 1.8 × 1.5m (6 × 5ft)
G 5 yrs: 1.5 × 0.9m (5 × 3ft)
Aspect: Best in full sun, in shelter.
Soil: Any good, fertile soil.
Lax, grassy foliage and tall, feather-duster creamy flowers in late summer and autumn.

Alternatives: *Deschampsia cespitosa* 'Bronzeschleier' (tufted hair grass); *Miscanthus sinensis* 'Gracillimus', *M. s.* 'Zebrinus'; *Molinia caerulea* subsp. *arundinacea* 'Transparent'; *Stipa gigantea* (golden oats, Spanish oats)

Yucca filamentosa (Adam's needle)
E HH Size: 1.8 × 1.8m (6 × 6ft)
G 5 yrs: 90 × 90cm (3 × 3ft)
Aspect: Full sun in a sheltered position.

Soil: Well-drained, dry fertile soil.
Long, narrow grey-green foliage, neither stiff nor sharp. Fragrant, cream flowers in summer.

Alternatives: *Agave americana* (century plant); *Cordyline australis* (cabbage tree, New Zealand cabbage palm); *Phormium* cvs (New Zealand flax, flax lily), *P. tenax*; *Trachycarpus fortunei* (syn. *Chamaerops excelsa*; Chusan palm, windmill palm)

Tiers and tears

These plants have horizontal or weeping habits: horizontal forms, appearing static, encourage the eye to move around on a level plane, while weeping shapes draw the eye down to ground level.

Cornus controversa 'Variegata' (wedding cake tree)
D HH Size: 6 × 5m (20 × 16ft)
G 5 yrs: 1.8 × 1.8m (6 × 6ft);
10yrs: 3 × 3m (10 × 10ft)
Aspect: Full sun or light shade in a sheltered position.
Soil: Deep, rich soil.
Growth ascends in horizontal tiers, a fine effect in winter. Soft, fluttering light green and white foliage.

Alternatives: *Cytisus* × *kewensis*; *Juniperus sabina* 'Tamariscifolia' ★; *Viburnum plicatum* 'Mariesii'

Pyrus salicifolia 'Pendula' (weeping willow-leaved pear)
E ★ HH Size: 6 × 4m (20 × 13ft)
G 5 yrs: 3 × 2.1m (10 × 7ft); 10yrs: 4 × 3m (13 × 10ft)
Aspect: Full sun, in a sheltered position.
Soil: Any, well-drained soil.
Narrow silver-grey foliage, and white flowers in late spring.

Alternatives: *Buddleja alternifolia* ★ (buddleia); *Itea ilicifolia*; *Salix* × *sepulcralis* var. *chrysocoma* (syn. S. 'Chrysocoma'; weeping willow)

Dramatic shape

This is an all-encompassing term for plants with a scene-stealing habit, form and foliage. Often termed architectural plants, they will draw your attention and demand inspection.

Aralia elata (Japanese angelica tree)
D HH Size: 3.5 × 3m (12 × 10ft)
G 5 yrs: 2.1 × 1.5m (7 × 5ft);
10yrs: 3 × 2.4m (10 × 8ft)
Aspect: Full sun. Provide shelter for best foliage.
Soil: Deep, fertile soil.
Huge fans of olive green foliage from spiny stems. Soft, flowering panicles in late summer. The variegated form is *A. e.* 'Variegata'.

Catalpa bignonioides 'Aurea' (golden Indian bean tree)
D ★ H Size: 4 × 4m (13 × 13ft)
G 5 yrs: 1.5 × 1.5m (5 × 5ft);
10yrs: 3 × 3m (10 × 10ft)
Aspect: Full sun, sheltered from strong winds.
Soil: Deep, rich soil.
Spreading habit with darkening stems and large, gold to lime green heart-shaped.

Cynara cardunculus (cardoon)
HH Size: 1.5m × 90cm (5 × 3ft)
G: should reach full size in one season
Aspect: Full sun in reasonable shelter
Soil: Deep, well-drained soil but tolerates dryness.
Hardy herbaceous perennial. Huge, silver-grey fans of deeply dissected, rough foliage. Insignificant mauve thistle heads.

Melianthus major (honey bush)
E NH/H Size: 3 × 3m 10 × 10ft)
G 5 yrs: 90 × 90cm (3 × 3ft);
10yrs: 2.1 × 2.1m (7 × 7ft)
Aspect: Full sun or very light shade in a sheltered site.
Soil: Deep, rich soil.
Large, curving and divided grey-green-blue foliage, glaucous in texture.

Alternatives: *Acanthus spinosus*; *Angelica archangelica*; *Fatsia japonica* ★ (see page 119); *Ferula communis* (giant fennel); *Gunnera manicata* (giant rhubarb); *Macleaya cordata* (syn. *Bocconia cordata*; tree celandine, plume poppy); *Musa basjoo* (syn. *M. japonica*; Japanese banana); *Rheum palmatum* 'Atrosanguineum'; *Thalia dealbata*; *Verbascum thapsus* 'Hagley Hybrid' (Aaron's rod)

Index

Acknowledgements

Author's acknowledgements

Special thanks to Caroline Ball, my editor, for her patient guidance; and also to Alan Hughes, my colleague, for his illustrations which convey exactly the feeling I was searching for to support the text. Thanks too, to Jenny Rogers, friend, and to Martyn, friend and partner, for being so generous with their time and advice.

Photograph acknowledgements

Jerry Harpur 4 (Anthony Sykes), 5 (Victor Nelson, New York), 8 (designer: Edwina von Gal, New York), 24 (designer: Christopher Masson, London), 31 right (designer: Robert Chittock, Seattle) 32 (designer: Paul Miles, Suffolk) 47 (designer: Jean Anderson), 48 (designer: Mel Watson, Los Angeles), 51 (designer: John Patrick, Melbourne), 52 (Freck Vreeland, Rome), 55 (Mel Light, Los Angeles), 57 (Christopher Masson, London) 63 (Clifton Landscape and Design, Harpers & Queen, RHS Chelsea 1996), 71 bottom (Old Rectory, Sudborough, Northants), 107 (designer: Hilary McMahon, RHS Chelsea), 114, Ron Simple, Philadelphia), 116 (designer: Simon Fraser, Hampton, Middlesex); **Marcus Harpur** 26 (designer: Jonathan Baillie, London), 35 (designer: Jonathan Baillie), 49 (designer: Jonathan Baillie), 78 (Jonathan Baillie), 95 (designer: Xa Tollemache, Evening Standard, RHS Chelsea 1997); **Anne Hyde** 14 (Andy Rees, garden designer, 1 Nup End Lane, Wingrave, Bucks), 16 (Vanessa and Vinda Saax, London E3), 24 (Chris Hubbard, Hitchin, Herts), 31 left (Mr and Mrs Coote, 40 Osler Rd, Oxford), 41 (Mr Tudway Quilter, Milton Lodge, Somerset), 61 (Mr and Mrs R. Sadler, Halfpenny Furze, Chalfont St Giles, Bucks), 64 (Peter Aldington, garden designer, Turn End, Haddenham, Bucks), 66 (Mr and Mrs Coote, 40 Osler Rd, Oxford), 68 (Chris Royffe, garden designer, Fieldhead, Boston Spa, Yorks), 72 (Mr J. Drake, Hardwicke House, Fen Ditton, Cambs), 73 bottom (Peter Aldington, garden designer, Turn End, Haddenham, Bucks), 73 top (Mr and Mrs C. Bott, Benington Lordship, Herts) 74 (H.M. the Queen, Sandringham, Norfolk), 81 (Lucy Somers, Queen Elizabeth Walk, London N16), 84 (Mr and Mrs R.A. Hammond, The Magnolias, Brentwood), 87 (Mary Payne, garden designer, Upper Stanton Drew, Bristol), 94 (Andy Rees, garden designer, 1 Nup End Lane, Wingrave, Bucks), 100 left (Beechfield, Wilts), 102 (Chris Royffe, garden designer, Fieldhead, Boston Spa, Yorks); **Andrew Lawson** 33 right (The Mosaic Garden, Melbourne, Australia), 37, 69, 83, 85 bottom, 93, 108 (RHS Chelsea 1996), 113; **Clive Nichols** 1 (designer: Sue Berger), 7 (designer: Sue Berger), 11 (designer: Roger Platts), 13 (designer: Christian Wright), 29 (designer: Julian Dowle), 33 left, 43 (The Old Rectory, Berks), 44 (Eastgrove Cottage, Worcs), 45 (designer: Christopher Pickard, RHS Chelsea 1997), 46 bottom (designer: Natural and Oriental Water Gardens, Hampton Court 1998), 59 (Jonathan Baillie), 71 top (designer: Alex Jefferson), 80 (designer: Sarah Eberle, Hampton Court 1998), 85 (Rosendal, Sweden), 99 (designer: Helen Dillon), 100 right (designer: Ann Frith), 103 (designer: Keeyla Meadows), 112; **Derek St Romaine** 34 (sculptor: Johnny Woodford), 39 (Mr and Mrs P. Carver, The Croft), 46 top, 82 designer: Simon Shire, RHS Chelsea 1997), 91 (designer: Julie Toll (RHS Chelsea 1995), 112 (designer: Barbara Hunt, Hampton Court 1994).